CHSPE Exam Study Guide

**CHSPE Practice Test Questions and Review for the
California High School Proficiency Exam**

FREE STRESS RELIEF BALL FROM TRIVIUM TEST PREP

Dear Customer,

Thank you for purchasing from Trivium Test Prep! Whether you're looking to join the military, get into college, or advance your career, we're honored to be a part of your journey.

To show our appreciation (and to help you relieve a little of that test-prep stress), we're offering a **FREE 5-Star Stress Relief Ball from Trivium Test Prep**. All we ask is that you email us your feedback and describe your experience with our product. Amazing, awful, or just so-so: we want to hear your thoughts!

To receive your **FREE 5-Star Stress Relief Ball from Trivium Test Prep**, please email us at 5star@triviumtestprep.com. Include "Free 5 Star" in the subject line and the following information in your email:

1. The title of the product you purchased.

2. Your rating from 1 – 5 (with 5 being the best).

3. Your feedback about the product, including how our materials helped you meet your goals and ways in which we can improve our products.

4. Your full name and shipping address so we can send your FREE 5-Star Stress Relief Ball.

If you have any questions or concerns please feel free to contact me directly.

Thank you, and good luck with your studies!

Alyssa Wagoner
Quality Control
alyssa.wagoner@triviumtestprep.com

Table of Contents

Introduction

Congratulations on your decision to take the California High School Proficiency Examination (CHSPE)! This test will assess your competency in high school-level Math, Reading, and Language; if you do well, you may be provided an exemption from high school – at the very least, you'll receive U.S. Department of Education and Federal Student Aid recognition for holding the equivalent of a high school diploma.

But let's not get ahead of ourselves. You've already made a great first step in purchasing this book – the next is to do well on the CHSPE.

What is the CHSPE?

The California High School Proficiency Examination (CHSPE) is a three-and-a-half hour exam, consisting of three sections: Math, Reading, and Language. The test is open to anyone over the age of sixteen, regardless of whether or not they are currently attending school. (A student under the age of sixteen may still take the CHSPE, but only if they have already completed the 10th grade.)

Anyone who takes and passes the CHSPE is awarded a Certificate of Proficiency from the State Board of Education; this certificate, as mentioned before, is recognized as the equivalent of a high school diploma.

> **Note!** Even if you pass the CHSPE, if you are under the age of eighteen, you are NOT exempt from attending school. If you pass the CHSPE, are under the age of eighteen, and wish to stop attending high school, then you are REQUIRED to have a guardian sign a waiver for you to leave school. More information can be found at the CHSPE website: http://www.chspe.net/about/.

Keep in mind that CHSPE stands for **California** High School Proficiency Examination. Many states outside of California do NOT recognize the CHSPE as a high school diploma-equivalent. So, if you are applying for college, a federal service job, etc. – that is outside of California – be sure to check out their individual requirements.

The Reading Section

- **54 Questions – Reading Comprehension**: Presents multiple short passages with corresponding questions.

- **30 Questions – Vocabulary**: Tests knowledge of word use and the ability to work with words.

The Language Section

- **48 Questions – Language**: Tests knowledge of basic grammar, punctuation, and sentence structure.

- **Essay**: Requires the composition of a short essay in response to a topic or prompt.

The Math Section

- **50 Questions – Mathematics**: Covers mathematical topics ranging in difficulty from basic operations to algebra and geometry. Requires knowledge of work equations, graphs, measurements and volume, percentages, averages, etc.

Scoring

Your score begins with a "raw" score, indicating how many questions were answered correctly. That raw score is then converted into a scaled score ranging from 250 to 450. (Scores are scaled because of the varying nature of the test. Some tests are more difficult than others; a scaled score balances things out.)

Generally (though again, it varies, so make sure to check whenever you take your test) if you can answer 65% or more of the questions correctly, then you will pass – definitely an attainable goal!

How This Book Works

The subsequent chapters in this book are divided into a review of those topics covered on the exam. This is not intended to "teach" or "re-teach" you these concepts – there is no way to cram all of that material into one book! Instead, we are going to help you recall all of the information which you've already learned. Even more importantly, we'll show you how to apply that knowledge.

Each chapter includes an extensive review, with practice drills at the end to test your knowledge. With time, practice, and determination, you'll be well-prepared for test day.

Chapter 1: Reading Comprehension

The Reading Section of the CHSPE is divided into two parts: Reading Comprehension and Vocabulary. The questions in the Reading Comprehension section are typically not overly difficult, but they do require the reader to pay close attention to every word. Skimming over even one word can completely change the meaning of a sentence, and result in the loss of a point.

There are three types of questions that you can encounter in the Reading Comprehension section of the CHSPE:

1. **About the Author**: The question will ask about the author's attitude, thoughts, opinions, etc. When encountering a question asking specifically about the author, pay attention to context clues in the article. The answer may not be explicitly stated, but instead conveyed in the overall message.

2. **Passage Facts**: You must distinguish between facts and opinions presented in the passage. Remember, a fact is something verifiable or proven, whereas an opinion is simply a belief that cannot be proven for sure. For example: "The sky is blue" is a fact that cannot be argued; "the sky is a prettier blue today than it was yesterday" is an opinion, since there is no scientific basis for what makes the sky "prettier" to a person.

3. **Additional Information**: These questions will have you look at what kind of information could be added to or was missing from the passage. They may also ask in what direction the passage was going. Questions may ask what statement could be added to strengthen the author's statement, or weaken it; they may also provide a fill-in-the-blank option to include a statement that is missing from, but fits with the rest of, the passage. When looking over answer choices, read them with the passage to see if they sound correct in context.

Strategies

Despite the different types of questions you will face, there are some strategies for Reading Comprehension which apply across the board:

- **Read the Answer Choices First**, then read the passage. This will save you time, as you will know what to look out for as you read.

- **Use the Process of Elimination**. Often at least one answer choice in a question is obviously incorrect. After reading the passage, eliminate any blatantly incorrect answer choices to increase your chances of finding the correct answer much more quickly.

- **Avoid "Negatives."** Generally, test-makers will not make negatives statements about anyone or anything. Statements will be either neutral or positive; so if it seems like an answer choice is making a negative connotation, it is very likely that the answer is intentionally false.

Here are some examples of the kinds of questions you may encounter in the Reading Comprehension section. Each passage will have at least one of the above listed question types – try to answer them for yourself before reading the solution. If you run into trouble, don't worry. We'll provide more practice drills later in the book, as well.

Sample One:

> *Exercise is a critical aspect for healthy development in children. Today, there is an epidemic of unhealthy children in the United States who will face health problems in adulthood due to poor diet and lack of exercise as children. This is a problem for all Americans, especially with the rising cost of health care.*
>
> *It is vital that school systems and parents encourage their children to engage in a minimum of 30 minutes of cardiovascular exercise each day, meaning their heart rate is mildly increased for sustained period. This is proven to decrease the likelihood of development diabetes, becoming obese, and a multitude of other health problems. Also, children need a proper diet rich in fruits and vegetables so that they can grow and development physically, as well as learn healthy eating habits early on.*

1. Which of the following describes the author's use of the word "vital"?
   a) Debatable.
   b) Very important .
   c) Somewhat important.
   d) Not important.
   e) Indicator.

Answer: This is an example of an "About the Author" question. You can tell, from both the tone and the intention of the article, that the author feels very strongly about the health of children and that action should be taken. Therefore, answer **b)** is the correct choice.

2. Which of the following is a fact in the passage, not an opinion?
   a) Fruits and vegetables are the best-tasting foods.
   b) Children today are lazier than they were in previous generations.
   c) The risk of diabetes in children is reduced by physical activity.
   d) Health care costs too much.
   e) Soccer is a better physical activity than tennis.

Answer: A fact is typically presented as a direct statement, not a comparison, which makes answer choice **c)** the correct answer. Notice that many of the incorrect answers contain words that can hint at it being an opinion such as "best," "better," "too much," or other comparisons. Also keep an eye out for answer choices that may be facts, but which are not stated in the passage.

3. What other information might the author have provided to strengthen the argument?
  a) Example of fruits and vegetables children should eat.
  b) How much health insurance costs today vs. 10 years ago.
  c) How many people live in the United States today.
  d) The rules of baseball and soccer.
  e) How many calories the average person burns by running 1 mile.

Answer: All of the choices would provide additional information, but only one pertains specifically to the improvement of health in children: choice **a)**.

Sample Two

1. Using the below Index, on which page would you find information on Organic Chemistry?

Science
    Geology: 110-124
    Astronomy: 126-137
    Physics: 140-159
    Chemistry: 161-170
    Biology: 171-179

Math
    Geometry: 201-209
    Calculus: 210-222
    Graphing: 225-251

  a) 210-222
  b) 225-251
  c) 126-137
  d) 161-170
  e) None of the above

Answer: The correct answer is choice **d)**. Pretty simple, huh? These types of questions are the easiest that you will find on the CHSPE. Simply look for key-words (in this case "Chemistry" is the only matching word), and then eliminate everything else that doesn't relate.

REVIEW: READING COMPREHENSION

This section will measure your ability to understand, analyze, and evaluate written passages. The passages will contain material from a variety of sources, and will cover a number of different topics.

Strategies

Despite the different types of questions you will face, there are some strategies for Reading Comprehension which apply across the board:

- Read the answer choices first, then read the passage. This will save you time, as you will know what to look out for as you read.

- Use the process of elimination. Some answer choices are obviously incorrect and are relatively easy to detect. After reading the passage, eliminate those blatantly incorrect answer choices; this increases your chance of finding the correct answer much more quickly.

- Avoid negative statements. Generally, test-makers will not make negative statements about anyone or anything. Statements will be either neutral or positive, so if it seems like an answer choice has a negative connotation, it is very likely that the answer is intentionally false.

The Main Idea

The main idea of a text is the purpose behind why a writer would choose to write a book, article, story, etc. Being able to find and understand the main idea is a critical skill necessary to comprehend and appreciate what you're reading.

Consider a political election. A candidate is running for office and plans to deliver a speech asserting her position on tax reform. The **topic** of the speech—tax reform—is clear to voters, and probably of interest to many. However, imagine that the candidate believes that taxes should be lowered. She is likely to assert this argument in her speech, supporting it with examples proving why lowering taxes would benefit the public and how it could be accomplished. While the topic of the speech would be tax reform, the benefit of lowering taxes would be the **main idea**. Other candidates may have different perspectives on the topic; they may believe that higher taxes are necessary, or that current taxes are adequate. It is likely that their speeches, while on the same topic of tax reform, would have different main ideas: different arguments likewise supported by different examples. Determining what a speaker, writer, or text is asserting about a specific issue will reveal the main idea.

One more quick note: the CHSPE may also ask about a passage's **theme**, which is similar to but distinct from its topic. While a topic is usually a specific *person, place, thing*, or *issue,* the theme is an *idea* or *concept* that the author refers back to frequently. Examples of common themes include ideas like the importance of family, the dangers of technology, and the beauty of nature.

There will be many questions on the CHSPE that require you to differentiate between the topic, theme, and main idea of a passage. Let's look at an example passage to see how you would answer these questions.

> **Example:** "Babe Didrikson Zaharias, one of the most decorated female athletes of the twentieth century, is an inspiration for everyone. Born in 1911 in Beaumont, Texas, Zaharias lived in a time when women were considered second-class to men, but she never let that stop her from becoming

a champion. Babe was one of seven children in a poor immigrant family, and was competitive from an early age. As a child she excelled at most things she tried, especially sports, which continued into high school and beyond. After high school, Babe played amateur basketball for two years, and soon after began training in track and field. Despite the fact that women were only allowed to enter in three events, Babe represented the United States in the 1932 Los Angeles Olympics, and won two gold medals and one silver for track and field events.

"In the early 1930s, Babe began playing golf which earned her a legacy. The first tournament she entered was a men's only tournament, however she did not make the cut to play. Playing golf as an amateur was the only option for a woman at this time, since there was no professional women's league. Babe played as an amateur for a little over a decade, until she turned pro in 1947 for the Ladies Professional Golf Association (LPGA) of which she was a founding member. During her career as a golfer, Babe won eighty-two tournaments, amateur and professional, including the U.S. Women's Open, All-American Open, and British Women's Open Golf Tournament. In 1953, Babe was diagnosed with cancer, but fourteen weeks later, she played in a tournament. That year she won her third U.S. Women's Open. However by 1955, she didn't have the physicality to compete anymore, and she died of the disease in 1956."

Determining the main idea, however, requires a little more analysis. The passage describes Babe Zaharias' life, but the main idea of the paragraph is what it says about her life. To figure out the main idea, consider what the writer is saying about Babe Zaharias. The writer is saying that she's someone to admire—that's the main idea and what unites all the information in the paragraph. Lastly, what might the theme of the passage be? The writer refers to several broad concepts, including never giving up and overcoming the odds, both of which could be themes for the passage. Two major indicators of the main idea of a paragraph or passage follow below:

- It is a general idea; it applies to all the more specific ideas in the passage. Every other sentence in a paragraph should be able to relate in some way to the main idea.

- It asserts a specific viewpoint that the author supports with facts, opinions, or other details. In other words, the main idea takes a stand.

Example: "From so far away it's easy to imagine the surface of our solar system's planets as enigmas—how could we ever know what those far-flung planets really look like? It turns out, however, that scientists have a number of tools at their disposal that allow them to paint detailed pictures of many planets' surfaces. The topography of Venus, for example, has been explored by several space probes, including the Russian Venera landers and NASA's Magellan orbiter. These craft used imaging and radar to map the surface of the planet, identifying a whole host of features including volcanoes, craters, and a complex system of channels. Mars has similarly been mapped by space probes, including the famous Mars Rovers, which are automated vehicles that actually landed on the surface of Mars. These rovers have been used by NASA and other space agencies to study the geology, climate, and possible biology of the planet.

"In addition these long-range probes, NASA has also used its series of orbiting telescopes to study distant planets. These four massively powerful telescopes include the famous Hubble Space Telescope as well as the Compton Gamma Ray Observatory, Chandra X-Ray Observatory, and the Spitzer Space Telescope. Scientists can use these telescopes to examine planets using not only visible light but also infrared and near-infrared light, ultraviolet light, x-rays and gamma rays.

"Powerful telescopes aren't just found in space: NASA makes use of Earth-bound telescopes as well. Scientists at the National Radio Astronomy Observatory in Charlottesville, VA, have spent decades using radio imaging to build an incredibly detailed portrait of Venus' surface. In fact, Earth-bound telescopes offer a distinct advantage over orbiting telescopes because they allow scientists to capture data from a fixed point, which in turn allows them to effectively compare data collected over long period of time."

Which of the following sentences best describes the main of the passage?
   a) It's impossible to know what the surfaces of other planets are really like.
   b) Telescopes are an important tool for scientists studying planets in our solar system.
   c) Venus' surface has many of the same features as the Earth's, including volcanoes, craters, and channels.
   d) Scientists use a variety of advanced technologies to study the surface of the planets in our solar system.

Answer a) can be eliminated because it directly contradicts the rest of the passage, which goes into detail about how scientists have learned about the surfaces of other planets. Answers b) and c) can also be eliminated because they offer only specific details from the passage—while both choices contain details from the passage, neither is general enough to encompass the passage as a whole. Only answer d) provides an assertion that is both backed up by the passage's content and general enough to cover the entire passage.

Topic and Summary Sentences

The main idea of a paragraph usually appears within the topic sentence. The **topic sentence** introduces the main idea to readers; it indicates not only the topic of a passage, but also the writer's perspective on the topic.

The first sentence in the Babe Zaharias text states the main idea: *Babe Didrikson Zaharias, one of the most decorated female athletes of the twentieth century, is an inspiration for everyone.*

Even though paragraphs generally begin with topic sentences due to their introductory nature, on occasion writers build up to the topic sentence by using supporting details in order to generate interest or build an argument. Be alert for paragraphs when writers do not include a clear topic sentence at all; even without a clear topic sentence, a paragraph will still have a main idea. You may also see a **summary sentence** at the end of a passage. As its name suggests, this sentence sums up the passage, often by restating the main idea and the author's key evidence supporting it.

Example: In the following paragraph, what are the topic and summary sentences?

"The Constitution of the United States establishes a series of limits to rein in centralized power. Separation of powers distributes federal authority among three competing branches: the executive, the legislative, and the judicial. Checks and balances allow the branches to check the usurpation of power by any one branch. States' rights are protected under the Constitution from too much encroachment by the federal government. Enumeration of powers names the specific and few powers the federal government has. These four restrictions have helped sustain the American republic for over two centuries."

The topic sentence is the first sentence in the paragraph. It introduces the topic of discussion, in this case the constitutional limits aimed at resisting centralized power. The summary sentence is the last sentence in the paragraph. It sums up the information that was just presented: here, that constitutional limits have helped sustain the United States of America for over two hundred years.

Implied Main Idea

When there's no clear topic sentence, you're looking for an **implied main idea**. This requires some detective work: you will need to look at the author's word choice and tone in addition to the content of the passage to find his or her main idea. Let's look at an example paragraph.

Example: "One of my summer reading books was *Mockingjay*. Though it's several hundred pages long, I read it in just a few days *I was captivated by the adventures of the main character and the complicated plot of the book. However, I felt like the ending didn't reflect the excitement of the story. Given what a powerful personality the main character has, I felt like the ending didn't do her justice.*"

Even without a clear topic sentence, this paragraph has a main idea. What is the writer's perspective on the book—what is the writer saying about it?
  a) *Mockingjay* is a terrific novel.
  b) *Mockingjay* is disappointing.
  c) *Mockingjay* is full of suspense.
  d) *Mockingjay* is a lousy novel.

The correct answer is B): the novel is disappointing. The process of elimination will reveal the correct answer if that is not immediately clear. While that the paragraph begins with positive commentary on the book—*I was captivated by the adventures of the main character and the complicated plot of the book*—this positive idea is followed by the contradictory transition word *however*. A) cannot be the correct answer because the author concludes that the novel was poor. Likewise, D) cannot be correct because it does not encompass all the ideas in the paragraph; despite the negative conclusion, the author enjoyed most of the book. The main idea should be able to encompass all of the thoughts in a paragraph; choice D) does not apply to the beginning of this paragraph. Finally, choice C) is too specific; it could only apply to the brief description of the plot and adventures of the main character. That leaves choice B) as the best option. The author initially enjoyed the book, but was disappointed by the ending, which seemed unworthy of the exciting plot and character.

Example: "Fortunately, none of Alyssa's coworkers has ever seen inside the large filing drawer in her desk. Disguised by the meticulous neatness of the rest of her workspace, there was no sign of the chaos beneath. To even open it, she had to struggle for several minutes with the enormous pile of junk jamming the drawer, until it would suddenly give way, and papers, folders, and candy wrappers spilled out of the top and onto the floor. It was an organizational nightmare, with torn notes and spreadsheets haphazardly thrown on top of each other, and melted candy smeared across pages. She was worried the odor would soon permeate to her coworker's desks, revealing to them her secret."

Which sentence best describes the main idea of the paragraph above?

  a) Alyssa wishes she could move to a new desk.
  b) Alyssa wishes she had her own office.
  c) Alyssa is glad none of her coworkers know about her messy drawer.
  d) Alyssa is sad because she doesn't have any coworkers.

Clearly, Alyssa has a messy drawer, and C) is the right answer. The paragraph begins by indicating her gratitude that her coworkers do not know about her drawer (*Fortunately, none of Alyssa's coworkers has ever seen inside the large filing drawer in her desk.*) Plus, notice how the drawer is described: *it was an organizational nightmare*, and it apparently doesn't even function properly: *to even open the drawer, she had to struggle for several minutes.* The writer reveals that it has an odor, with *melted candy* inside. Alyssa is clearly ashamed of her drawer and fearful of being judged by her coworkers for it.

Supporting Details

Supporting details provide more support for the author's main idea. For instance, in the Babe Zaharias example above, the writer makes the general assertion that *Babe Didrikson Zaharias, one of the most decorated female athletes of the twentieth century, is an inspiration for everyone.* The rest of the paragraph provides supporting details with facts showing why she is an inspiration: the names of the illnesses she overcame, and the specific years she competed in the Olympics.

Be alert for **signal words**, which can be helpful in identifying supporting details. Signal words can also help you rule out sentences that are too broad to be the main idea or topic sentence: if a sentence begins with a signal word, it will likely be too specific to be a main idea.

Questions on the CHSPE will ask you to do two things with supporting details: you will need to find details that support a particular idea and also explain why a particular detail was included in the passage. In order to answer these questions, you need to have a solid understanding of the passage's main idea. With this knowledge, you can determine how a supporting detail fits in with the larger structure of the passage.

Example: "From so far away it's easy to imagine the surface of our solar system's planets as enigmas—how could we ever know what those far-flung planets really look like? It turns out, however, that scientists have a number of tools at their disposal that allow them to paint detailed pictures of many planets' surfaces. The topography of Venus, for example, has been explored by several space probes, including the Russian *Venera* landers and NASA's *Magellan* orbiter. These craft used imaging and radar to map the surface of the planet, identifying a whole host of features including volcanoes, craters, and a complex system of channels. Mars has similarly been mapped by space probes, including the famous Mars Rovers, which are automated vehicles that actually landed on the surface of Mars. These rovers have been used by NASA and other space agencies to study the geology, climate, and possible biology of the planet.

"In addition these long-range probes, NASA has also used its series of orbiting telescopes to study distant planets. These four massively powerful telescopes include the famous Hubble Space Telescope as well as the Compton Gamma Ray Observatory, Chandra X-Ray Observatory, and the Spitzer Space Telescope. Scientists can use these telescopes to examine planets using not only visible light but also infrared and near-infrared light, ultraviolet light, x-rays and gamma rays.

"Powerful telescopes aren't just found in space: NASA makes use of Earth-bound telescopes as well. Scientists at the National Radio Astronomy Observatory in Charlottesville, VA, have spent decades using radio imaging to build an incredibly detailed portrait of Venus' surface. In fact, Earth-bound telescopes offer a distinct advantage over orbiting telescopes because they allow scientists to capture data from a fixed point, which in turn allows them to effectively compare data collected over long period of time."

Which sentence from the text best helps develop the idea that scientists make use of many different technologies to study the surfaces of other planets?

    a) These rovers have been used by NASA and other space agencies to study the geology, climate, and possible biology of the planet.

    b) From so far away it's easy to imagine the surface of our solar system's planets as enigmas—how could we ever know what those far-flung planets really look like?

    c) In addition these long-range probes, NASA has also used its series of orbiting telescopes to study distant planets.

    d) These craft used imaging and radar to map the surface of the planet, identifying a whole host of features including volcanoes, craters, and a complex system of channels.

You're looking for detail from the passage that supports the main idea—scientists make use of many different technologies to study the surfaces of other planets. Answer a) includes a specific detail about rovers, but does not offer any details that support the idea of multiple technologies being used. Similarly, answer d) provides another specific detail about space probes. Answer b) doesn't provide any supporting details; it simply introduces the topic of the passage. Only answer c) provides a detail that directly supports the author's assertion that scientists use multiple technologies to study the planets.

If true, which detail could be added to the passage above to support the author's argument that scientists use many different technologies to study the surface of planets?

    a) Because the Earth's atmosphere blocks x-rays, gamma rays, and infrared radiation, NASA needed to put telescopes in orbit above the atmosphere.

    b) In 2015, NASA released a map of Venus which was created by compiling images from orbiting telescopes and long-range space probes.

    c) NASA is currently using the *Curiosity* and *Opportunity* rovers to look for signs of ancient life on Mars.

    d) NASA has spent over $2.5 billion to build, launch, and repair the Hubble Space Telescope.

You can eliminate answers c) and d) because they don't address the topic of studying the surface of planets. Answer a) can also be eliminated because it only addresses a single technology. Only choice b) provides would add support to the author's claim about the importance of using multiple technologies.

The author likely included the detail *Earth-bound telescopes offer a distinct advantage over orbiting telescopes because they allow scientists to capture data from a fixed point* in order to:

    a) Explain why it has taken scientists so long to map the surface of Venus.

    b) Suggest that Earth-bound telescopes are the most important equipment used by NASA scientists.

    c) Prove that orbiting telescopes will soon be replaced by Earth-bound telescopes.

    d) Demonstrate why NASA scientists rely on my different types of scientific equipment.

Only answer d) directs directly to the author's main argument. The author doesn't mention how long it has taken to map the surface of Venus (answer a), nor does he say that one technology is more important than the others (answer b). And while this detail does highlight the advantages of using Earth-bound telescopes, the author's argument is that many technologies are being used at the same time, so there's no reason to think that orbiting telescopes will be replaced (answer c).

Text Structure

Authors can structure passages in a number of different ways. These distinct organizational patterns, referred to as **text structure**, use the logical relationships between ideas to improve the readability and coherence of a text. The most common ways passages are organized include:

- **problem-solution**: the author presents a problem and then discusses a solution

- **comparison-contrast**: the author presents two situations and then discusses the similarities and differences

- **cause-effect**: the author presents an action and then discusses the resulting effects

- **descriptive**: an idea, object, person, or other item is described in detail

Example: "The issue of public transportation has begun to haunt the fast-growing cities of the southern United States. Unlike their northern counterparts, cities like Atlanta, Dallas, and Houston have long promoted growth out and not up—these are cities full of sprawling suburbs and single-family homes, not densely concentrated skyscrapers and apartments. What to do then, when all those suburbanites need to get into the central business districts for work? For a long time it seemed highways were the answer: twenty-lane wide expanses of concrete that would allow commuters to move from home to work and back again. But these modern miracles have become time-sucking, pollution spewing nightmares. They may not like it, but it's time for these cities to turn toward public transport like trains and buses if they want their cities to remain livable."

The organization of this passage can best be described as:
   a) a comparison of two similar ideas
   b) a description of a place
   c) a discussion of several effects all related to the same cause
   d) a discussion of a problem followed by the suggestion of a solution

You can exclude answer choice c) because the author provides no root cause or a list of effects. From there this question gets tricky, because the passage contains structures similar to those described above. For example, it compares two things (cities in the North and South) and describes a place (a sprawling city). However, if you look at the overall organization of the passage, you can see that it starts by presenting a problem (transportation) and then presents a solution (trains and buses), making answer d) the only choice that encompasses the entire passage.

The Author's Purpose

Whenever an author writes a text, she always has a purpose, whether that's to entertain, inform, explain, or persuade. A short story, for example, is meant to entertain, while an online news article would be designed to inform the public about a current event.

Each of these different types of writing has a specific name. On the CHSPE, you will be asked to identify which of these categories a passage fits into:

- **Narrative writing** tells a story. (novel, short story, play)

- **Expository writing** informs people. (newspaper and magazine articles)

- **Technical writing** explains something. (product manual, directions)

- **Persuasive writing** tries to convince the reader of something. (opinion column on a blog)

You may also be asked about primary and secondary sources. These terms describe not the writing itself but the author's relationship to what's being written about. A **primary source** is an unaltered piece of writing that was composed during the time when the events being described took place; these texts are often written by the people involved. A **secondary source** might address the same topic but provides extra commentary or analysis. These texts can be written by people not directly involved in the events. For example, a book written by a political candidate to inform people about his or her stand on an issue is a primary source; an online article written by a journalist analyzing how that position will affect the election is a secondary source.

> **Example:** "Elizabeth closed her eyes and braced herself on the armrests that divided her from her fellow passengers. Take-off was always the worst part for her. The revving of the engines, the way her stomach dropped as the plane lurched upward: it made her feel sick. Then, she had to watch the world fade away beneath her, getting smaller and smaller until it was just her and the clouds hurtling through the sky. Sometimes (but only sometimes) it just had to be endured, though. She focused on the thought of her sister's smiling face and her new baby nephew as the plane slowly pulled onto the runway."
>
> The passage above is reflective of which type of writing?
> a) Narrative
> b) Expository
> c) Technical
> d) Persuasive

The passage is telling a story—we meet Elizabeth and learn about her fear of flying—so it's a narrative text (answer a). There is no factual information presented or explained, nor is the author trying to persuade the reader.

Facts vs. Opinions

On the CHSPE Reading passages you might be asked to identify a statement in a passage as either a fact or an opinion, so you'll need to know the difference between the two. A **fact** is a statement or thought that can be proven to be true. The statement *Wednesday comes after Tuesday* is a fact—you can point to a calendar to prove it. In contrast, an **opinion** is an assumption that is not based in fact and cannot be proven to be true. The assertion that *television is more entertaining than feature films* is an opinion—people will disagree on this, and there's no reference you can use to prove or disprove it.

Example:
"Exercise is critical for healthy development in children. Today, there is an epidemic of unhealthy children in the United States who will face health problems in adulthood due to poor diet and lack of exercise as children. This is a problem for all Americans, especially with the rising cost of healthcare.

"It is vital that school systems and parents encourage their children to engage in a minimum of thirty minutes of cardiovascular exercise each day, mildly increasing their heart rate for a sustained period. This is proven to decrease the likelihood of developmental diabetes, obesity, and a multitude of other health problems. Also, children need a proper diet rich in fruits and vegetables so that they can grow and develop physically, as well as learn healthy eating habits early on."

Which of the following is a fact in the passage, not an opinion?
  a) Fruits and vegetables are the best way to help children be healthy.
  b) Children today are lazier than they were in previous generations.
  c) The risk of diabetes in children is reduced by physical activity.
  d) Children should engage in thirty minutes of exercise a day.

Choice b) can be discarded immediately because it is negative and is not discussed anywhere in the passage. Answers a) and d) are both opinions—the author is promoting exercise, fruits, and vegetables as a way to make children healthy. (Notice that these incorrect answers contain words that hint at being an opinion such as *best*, *should*, or other comparisons.) Answer b), on the other hand, is a simple fact stated by the author; it's introduced by the word *proven* to indicate that you don't need to just take the author's word for it.

Drawing Conclusions

In addition to understanding the main idea and factual content of a passage, you'll also be asked to take your analysis one step further and anticipate what other information could logically be added to the passage. In a non-fiction passage, for example, you might be asked which statement the author of the passage would agree with. In an excerpt from a fictional work, you might be asked to anticipate what the character would do next.

To answer these questions, you need to have a solid understanding of the topic, theme, and main idea of the passage; armed with this information, you can figure out which of the answer choices best fits within those criteria (or alternatively, which ones do not). For example, if the author of the passage is advocating for safer working conditions in textile factories, any supporting details that would be added to the passage should support that idea. You might add sentences that contain information about the number of accidents that occur in textile factories or that outline a new plan for fire safety.

Example: "Today, there is an epidemic of unhealthy children in the United States who will face health problems in adulthood due to poor diet and lack of exercise during their childhood. This is a problem for all Americans, as adults with chronic health issues are adding to the rising cost of healthcare. A child who grows up living an unhealthy lifestyle is likely to become an adult who does the same.

"Because exercise is critical for healthy development in children, it is vital that school systems and parents encourage their children to engage in a minimum of thirty minutes of cardiovascular exercise each day. Even this small amount of exercise has been proven to decrease the likelihood that young people will develop diabetes, obesity, and other health issues as adults. In addition to exercise, children need a proper diet rich in fruits and vegetables so that they can grow and develop physically. Starting a good diet early also teaches children healthy eating habits they will carry into adulthood."

The author of this passage would most likely agree with which statement?
   a) Parents are solely responsible for the health of their children.
   b) Children who do not want to exercise should not be made to.
   c) Improved childhood nutrition will help lower the amount Americans spend on healthcare.
   d) It's not important to teach children healthy eating habits because they will learn them as adults.

The author would most likely support answer c): he mentions in the first paragraph that unhealthy habits are adding to the rising cost of healthcare. The main idea of the passage is that nutrition and exercise are important for children, so answer b) doesn't make sense—the author would likely support measures to encourage children to exercise. Answers a) and d) can also be eliminated because they are directly contradicted in the text. The author specifically mentions the role of schools systems, so he doesn't believe parents are solely responsible for their children's health. He also specifically states that children who grow up with unhealthy habit will become adults with unhealthy habits, which contradicts d).

Example: "Elizabeth closed her eyes and braced herself on the armrests that divided her from her fellow passengers. Take-off was always the worst part for her. The revving of the engines, the way her stomach dropped as the plane lurched upward: it made her feel sick. Then, she had to watch the world fade away beneath her, getting smaller and smaller until it was just her and the clouds hurtling through the sky. Sometimes (but only sometimes) it just had to be endured, though. She focused on the thought of her sister's smiling face and her new baby nephew as the plane slowly pulled onto the runway."

Which of the following is Elizabeth least likely to do in the future?
   a) Take a flight to her brother's wedding.
   b) Apply for a job as a flight attendant.
   c) Never board an airplane again.
   d) Get sick on an airplane.

It's clear from the passage that Elizabeth hates flying, but it willing to endure it for the sake of visiting her family. Thus, it seems likely that she would be willing to get on a plane for her brother's wedding, making a) and c) incorrect answers. The passage also explicitly tells us that she feels sick on planes, so d) is likely to happen. We can infer, though, that she would not enjoy being on an airplane for work, so she's very unlikely to apply for a job as a flight attendant, which is choice b).

Test Your Knowledge: Reading Comprehension

Remember to read the questions first, make sure that you read ALL answer choices ALL THE WAY THROUGH, and use process of elimination to make your job of selecting the correct answer easier. If you can answer a majority of these questions correctly, you are likely ready for the Reading Section of the CHSPE.

Read each of the following paragraphs carefully and answer the questions that follow.

The Flu
Influenza, or the flu, has historically been one of the most common and deadliest human sicknesses. While many people who contract this virus will recover, others will not. Over the past 150 years, tens of millions of people have died from the flu, and millions more have been left with lingering complications including secondary infections.

Although it's a common disease, the flu is actually not highly infectious; that is, it is relatively difficult to contract. The virus can only be transmitted when individuals come into direct contact with the bodily fluids of people infected with it, often when they are exposed to expelled aerosol particles resulting from coughing and sneezing. Since these particles only travel short distances and the virus will die within a few hours on hard surfaces, it can be contained with simple health measures like hand washing and face masks. However, the spread of this disease can only be contained when people are aware that such measures must be taken. One of the reasons the flu has historically been so deadly is the window of time between a person's infection and the development of symptoms. Viral shedding—when the body releases a virus that has been successfully reproducing in it—takes place two days after infection, while symptoms do not usually develop until the third day. Thus, infected individuals may unknowingly infect others for least twenty-four hours before developing symptoms themselves.

1. What is the main idea of the passage?
   a) The flu is a deadly disease that's difficult to control because people become infectious before they show symptoms.
   b) In order for the flu to be transmitted, individuals must come in contact with bodily fluids from infected individuals.
   c) The spread of flu is easy to contain because the virus does not live long either as aerosol particles or on hard surfaces.
   d) The flu has killed tens of millions of people and can often cause deadly secondary infections.

2. Why isn't the flu considered to be highly infectious?
   a) Many people who get the flu will recover and have no lasting complications, so only a small number of people who become infected will die.
   b) The process of viral shedding takes two days, so infected individuals have enough time to implement simple health measures that stop the spread of the disease.
   c) The flu virus cannot travel far or live for long periods of time outside the human body, so its spread can easily be contained if measures are taken.
   d) Twenty-four hours is a relatively short period of time for the virus to spread among a population.

3. Which of the following correctly describes the flu?
    a) The flu is easy to contract and always fatal.
    b) The flu is difficult to contract and always fatal.
    c) The flu is easy to contract and sometimes fatal.
    d) The flu is difficult to contract and sometimes fatal.

4. Which statement is not a detail from the passage?
    a) Tens of millions of people have been killed by the flu virus.
    b) There is typically a twenty-four hour window during which individuals are infectious but not showing flu symptoms.
    c) Viral shedding is the process by which people recover from the flu.
    d) The flu can be transmitted by direct contact with bodily fluids from infected individuals or by exposure to aerosol particles.

5. What is the meaning of the word *measures* in the last paragraph?
    a) a plan of action
    b) a standard unit
    c) an adequate amount
    d) a rhythmic movement

6. What can the reader conclude from the passage above?
    a) Preemptively implementing health measures like hand washing and face masks could help stop the spread of the flu virus.
    b) Doctors are not sure how the flu virus is transmitted, so they are unsure how to stop it from spreading.
    c) The flu is dangerous because it is both deadly and highly infectious.
    d) Individuals stop being infectious three days after they are infected.

Snakes

Skin coloration and markings play an important role in the world of snakes. Those intricate diamonds, stripes, and swirls help these animals hide from predators and attract mates. Perhaps most importantly (for us humans, anyway), the markings can also indicate whether a snake is venomous. While it might seem counterintuitive for a poisonous snake to stand out in bright red or blue, that fancy costume tells any approaching predator that eating it would be a bad idea.

If you see a flashy-looking snake out the woods, though, those markings don't necessarily mean it's poisonous: some snakes have a found a way to ward off predators without the actual venom. The California king snake, for example, has very similar markings to the venomous coral snake with whom it frequently shares a habitat. However, the king snake is actually nonvenomous; it's merely pretending to be dangerous to eat. A predatory hawk or eagle, usually hunting from high in the sky, can't tell the difference between the two species, so the king snake gets passed over and lives another day.

7. What is the author's primary purpose in writing this essay?
    a) to explain how the markings on a snake are related to whether it is venomous
    b) to teach readers the difference between coral snakes and king snakes
    c) to illustrate why snakes are dangerous
    d) to demonstrate how animals survive in difficult environments

8. What can the reader conclude from the passage above?
   a) The king snake is dangerous to humans.
   b) The coral snake and the king snake are both hunted by the same predators.
   c) It's safe to handle snakes in the woods because you can easily tell whether they're poisonous.
   d) The king snake changes its markings when hawks or eagles are close by.

9. What is the best summary of this passage?
   a) Humans can use coloration and markings to determine whether snakes are poisonous.
   b) Animals often use coloration and markings to attract mates and warn predators that they're poisonous.
   c) The California king snake and coral snake have nearly identical markings.
   d) Venomous snakes often have bright markings, although nonvenomous snakes can also mimic those colors.

10. Which statement is not a detail from the passage?
    a) Predators will avoid eating king snakes because their markings are similar to those on coral snakes.
    b) King snakes and coral snakes live in the same habitats.
    c) The coral snake uses its coloration to hide from predators.
    d) The king snake is not venomous.

11. What is the meaning of the word *intricate* in the first paragraph?
    a) complicated
    b) colorful
    c) purposeful
    d) changeable

12. What is the difference between king snakes and coral snakes according to the passage?
    a) Both king snakes and coral snakes are nonvenomous, but coral snakes have colorful markings.
    b) Both king snakes and coral snakes are venomous, but king snakes have colorful markings.
    c) King snakes are nonvenomous, while coral snakes are venomous.
    d) Coral snakes are nonvenomous, while king snakes are venomous.

Popcorn

Popcorn is often associated with fun and festivities, both in and out of the home. We eat it in theaters, smothering it in butter, and at home, fresh from the microwave. But popcorn isn't just for fun—it's also a multimillion-dollar industry with a long and fascinating history.

While popcorn might seem like a modern invention, its history actually dates back thousands of years, making it one of the oldest snack foods enjoyed around the world. Popping is believed by food historians to be one of the earliest uses of cultivated corn. In 1948, Herbert Dick and Earle Smith discovered old popcorn dating back 4000 years in the New Mexico Bat Cave. For the Aztecs who called the caves home, popcorn (or *momochitl*) played an important role in society, both as a food staple and in ceremonies. The Aztecs cooked popcorn by heating sand in a fire; when it was heated, kernels were added and would pop when exposed to the heat of the sand.

The American love affair with popcorn began in 1912, when it was first sold in theaters. The popcorn industry flourished during the Great Depression by advertising popcorn as a wholesome and economical food. Selling for five to ten cents a bag, it was a luxury that the downtrodden could afford. With the introduction of mobile popcorn machines at the World's Columbian Exposition, popcorn moved from the theater into fairs and parks. Popcorn continued to rule the snack food kingdom until the rise in popularity of home televisions during the 1950s.

The popcorn industry quickly reacted to its decline in sales by introducing pre-popped and un-popped popcorn for home consumption. However, it wasn't until microwave popcorn became commercially available in 1981 that at-home popcorn consumption began to grow exponentially. With the wide availability of microwaves in the United States, popcorn also began popping up in offices and hotel rooms. The home still remains the most popular popcorn eating spot, though: today, seventy percent of the sixteen billion quarts of popcorn consumed annually in the United States is eaten at home.

13. What can the reader conclude from the passage above?
   a) People ate less popcorn in the 1950s than in previous decades because they went to the movies less.
   b) Without mobile popcorn machines, people would not have been able to eat popcorn during the Great Depression.
   c) People enjoyed popcorn during the Great Depression because it was a luxury food.
   d) During the 1800s, people began abandoning theaters to go to fairs and festivals.

14. What is the author's primary purpose in writing this essay?
   a) to explain how microwaves affected the popcorn industry
   b) to show that popcorn, while popular in American history, is older than many people realize
   c) to illustrate the global history of popcorn from ancient cultures to modern times
   d) to demonstrate the importance of popcorn in various cultures

15. Which of the following is not a fact stated in the passage?
   a) Archaeologists have found popcorn dating back 4000 years.
   b) Popcorn was first sold in theatres in 1912.
   c) Consumption of popcorn dropped in 1981 with the growth in popularity of home televisions.
   d) Seventy percent of the popcorn consumed in the United States is eaten in homes.

16. What is the best summary of this passage?
   a) Popcorn is a popular snack food that dates back thousands of years. Its popularity in the United States has been tied to the development of theatres and microwaves.
   b) Popcorn has been a popular snack food for thousands of years. Archaeologists have found evidence that many ancient cultures used popcorn as a food staple and in ceremonies.
   c) Popcorn was first introduced in America in 1912, and its popularity has grown exponentially since then. Today, over sixteen billion quarts of popcorn are consumed in the United States annually.
   d) Popcorn is a versatile snack food that can be eaten with butter and other toppings. It can also be cooked in a number of different ways, including in microwaves.

Test Your Knowledge: Reading Comprehension – Answers

1. a)

2. c)

3. d)

4. c)

5. a)

6. a)

7. a)

8. b)

9. d)

10. c)

11. a)

12. c)

13. a)

14. b)

15. c)

16. a)

Chapter 2: Vocabulary

The next part of the Reading Section of the CHSPE is the Vocabulary section, which will consist of 30 multiple choice questions. These questions will require you to choose: the proper definition of a word (or words) in a sentence; the best description of how a word relates to the sentence; or the word that best belongs in a sentence.

The good news is that you have been answering these types of questions since you first learned to read and write. Different forms of sentence completion questions are used for tests and quizzes in all subject areas, which is one of the reasons they are used on the CHSPE. Don't worry - you won't be expected to know every word in the English language, but you are expected to know a good percentage of commonly-tested words.

Strategies

1. Read the sentence through entirely and say "blank" when you come upon a blank in the sentence. This will give you, not only a feel of the language being used, but the chance to identify any context clues which may help identify the correct choice. We'll go over context clues later in the review.

2. Don't memorize lists of vocabulary. Most students will simply study thousands of new words and their definitions – this is a huge mistake! The test will not provide a list of words and their definitions to match. You will be tested on how words are *used* within a sentence.

   It's important to study in the way you will be tested. Therefore, in order to maximize your score, practice using the words you are learning in sentences, whether by writing and/or conversing with them (doing both is highly recommended). That way, the words will become familiar to you.

   One way to study for this section is to write down 20 new words at the beginning of the week. By the end of the week, you must use all the words on the list in a comprehensive paragraph. (This also helps with the writing section.)

3. Learn the meanings of common word prefixes, suffixes, and root words. We'll review these as well.

4. Read the sentence and answer choices carefully. Just as with reading comprehension, a single detail in a sentence can completely change the meaning.

5. Reread the sentence with your answer choice; does it sound right?

6. If you are still unsure, try to narrow down a couple of answer choices through the process of elimination. Then, make an educated guess.

REVIEW: VOCABULARY

Meaning of Words and Phrases

On the Reading section you may also be asked to provide definitions or intended meanings for words within passages. You may have never encountered some of these words before the test, but there are tricks you can use to figure out what they mean.

Context Clues

The most fundamental vocabulary skill is using the context in which a word is used to determine its meaning. Your ability to observe sentences closely is extremely useful when it comes to understanding new vocabulary words.

There are two types of context that can help you understand the meaning of unfamiliar words: situational context and sentence context. Regardless of which context is present, these types of questions are not really testing your knowledge of vocabulary; rather, they test your ability to comprehend the meaning of a word through its usage.

Situational context is context that is presented by the setting or circumstances in which a word or phrase occurs. **Sentence context** occurs within the specific sentence that contains the vocabulary word. To figure out words using sentence context clues, you should first determine the most important words in the sentence.

There are four types of clues that can help you understand context, and therefore the meaning of a word:

- **Restatement** clues occur when the definition of the word is clearly stated in the sentence.

- **Positive/negative clues** can tell you whether a word has a positive or negative meaning.

- **Contrast clues** include the opposite meaning of a word. Words like *but, on the other hand*, and *however* are tip-offs that a sentence contains a contrast clue.

- **Specific detail clues** provide a precise detail that can illuminate the word's meaning.

It is important to remember that more than one of these clues can be present in the same sentence. The more there are, the easier it will be to determine the meaning of the word. For example, the following sentence uses both restatement and positive/negative clues: *Janet suddenly found herself destitute, so poor she could barely afford to eat*. The second part of the sentence clearly indicates that *destitute* is a negative word. It also restates the meaning: very poor.

> **Example:** I had a hard time reading her *illegible* handwriting.
> - a) neat
> - b) unsafe
> - c) sloppy
> - d) educated

Already, you know that this sentence is discussing something that is hard to read. Look at the word that *illegible* is describing: handwriting. Based on context clues, you can tell that *illegible* means that her handwriting is hard to read.

Next, look at the answer choices. Choice a), *neat,* is obviously a wrong answer because neat handwriting would not be difficult to read. Choices b) and d), *unsafe* and *educated,* don't make sense. Therefore, choice c), *sloppy,* is the best answer.

Example: The dog was *dauntless* in the face of danger, braving the fire to save the girl trapped inside the building.
- a) difficult
- b) fearless
- c) imaginative
- d) startled

Demonstrating bravery in the face of danger would be b) *fearless*. In this case, the restatement clue (*braving the fire*) tells you exactly what the word means.

Example: Beth did not spend any time preparing for the test, but Tyrone kept a *rigorous* study schedule.
- a) strict
- b) loose
- c) boring
- d) strange

In this case, the contrast word *but* tells us that Tyrone studied in a different way than Beth, which means it's a contrast clue. If Beth did not study hard, then Tyrone did. The best answer, therefore, is choice a).

Analyzing Words

As you no doubt know, determining the meaning of a word can be more complicated than just looking in a dictionary. A word might have more than one **denotation**, or definition; which one the author intends can only be judged by looking at the surrounding text. For example, the word *quack* can refer to the sound a duck makes, or to a person who publicly pretends to have a qualification which he or she does not actually possess.

A word may also have different **connotations**, which are the implied meanings and emotion a word evokes in the reader. For example, a cubicle is a simply a walled desk in an office, but for many the word implies a constrictive, uninspiring workplace. Connotations can vary greatly between cultures and even between individuals.

Lastly, authors might make use of **figurative language**, which is the use of a word to imply something other than the word's literal definition. This is often done by comparing two things. If you say *I felt like a butterfly when I got a new haircut*, the listener knows you don't resemble an insect but instead felt beautiful and transformed.

Word Structure

Although you are not expected to know every word in the English language for your test, you will need the ability to use deductive reasoning to find the choice that is the best match for the word in question, which is why we are going to explain how to break a word into its parts to determine its meaning. Many words can be broken down into three main parts:

prefix – root – suffix

Roots are the building blocks of all words. Every word is either a root itself or has a root. Just as a plant cannot grow without roots, neither can vocabulary, because a word must have a root to give it meaning. The root is what is left when you strip away all the prefixes and suffixes from a word. For example, in the word *unclear*, if you take away the prefix *un-*, you have the root *clear*.

Roots are not always recognizable words, because they generally come from Latin or Greek words, such as *nat*, a Latin root meaning born. The word *native*, which means a person born in a referenced placed, comes from this root, so does the word *prenatal*, meaning before birth. It's important to keep in mind, however, that roots do not always match the exact definitions of words, and they can have several different spellings.

A **Prefix** is a syllable(s) added to the beginning of a word, while **suffixes** are syllables added to the end of the word. Both carry assigned meanings and can be attached to a word to completely change the word's meaning or to enhance the word's original meaning.

The word *prefix* itself can serve as an example: *fix* means to place something securely and *pre-* means before. Therefore, *prefix* means to place something before or in front. Now let's look at a suffix: in the word *feminism*, *femin* is a root which means female. The suffix *-ism* means act, practice, or process. Thus, *feminism* is the process of establishing equal rights for women.

Although you cannot determine the meaning of a word by a prefix or suffix alone, you can use this knowledge to eliminate answer choices; understanding if a word has a positive or negative connotation can give you the partial meaning of the word.

Test Your Knowledge: Vocabulary

For the following questions, select the answer choice with the word or words that best fit in the sentence.

1. The investor seemed almost_____: she knew which stocks to select before they rose in value.
   a) Circumspect
   b) Prescient
   c) Audacious
   d) Discerning
   e) Obtuse

2. The team of biologists was well prepared for the _____ climate in which they would be working; the tents and clothing they brought were all _____ to water.
   a) Equatorial…Impervious
   b) Arid…Impenetrable
   c) Humid…Porous
   d) Parched…Repulsive
   e) Tempestuous…Susceptible

3. Library cataloguing systems have always been important in _____ vast collections of knowledge; however, as information is increasingly_____, methods of organizing it are changing.
   a) Organizing…Diminished
   b) Documenting…Depleted
   c) Confounding…Uploaded
   d) Systematizing…Digitized
   e) Collating…Proliferated

4. Linda went to the meeting on the _____ of hearing about the new plan; in reality, she went because she wanted to spend some time away from her desk.
   a) Hunch
   b) Rationale
   c) Pretext
   d) Motive
   e) Deception

5. If elected, the candidate's first priority would be to ____ the laws which were negatively affecting his constituency.
   a) Allay
   b) Sanction
   c) Abrogate
   d) Ratify
   e) Lampoon

6. The chefs disagreed about the effect of an unusual spice in the dish; one felt that it added ____ to an otherwise standard meal, while the other maintained that it ____ the cuisine.
    a) Pungency…Ravaged
    b) Relish…Augmented
    c) Redolence…Buttressed
    d) Drivel…Rectified
    e) Zest…Undermined

7. It is important to think _____ when learning about a new place because the culture, history, geography, and politics all interact to enable true understanding.
    a) Discordantly
    b) Discretely
    c) Critically
    d) Holistically
    e) Authentically

8. Astronomers in the 15th century were not using the types of _____ instruments we have today; rather, they successfully _____ the distances between planetary bodies using observations and what they understood about physics on Earth.
    a) Precise…Deduced
    b) Redundant…Concluded
    c) Meticulous…Appraised
    d) Efficacious…Promulgated
    e) Sophisticated…Generalized

9. In order to _____ the tradition, the family members made an effort to _____ the younger generation in the way that they had done it in the past.
    a) Nullify…Assuage
    b) Extend…Indoctrinate
    c) Formalize…Assimilate
    d) Deemphasize…Edify
    e) Perpetuate…Instruct

10. The play had a(n) _____ tone; all the patrons left the theater chortling and pleased.
    a) Ecstatic
    b) Jovial
    c) Somber
    d) Analytic
    e) Melancholy

11. Jeff was absolutely _____ about his idea; try as we might, we could not dissuade him.
    a) Parsimonious
    b) Relenting
    c) Adamant
    d) Pragmatic
    e) Capricious

12. In weaving cloth with threads, one draws the weft, or horizontal yarns, through the warp yarns, or the vertical, in an even and _____ manner to create a tight cloth.
    a) Consistent
    b) Oblique
    c) Imaginative
    d) Wholesome
    e) Substantial

13. College students quickly learn that _____ can be much more valuable than _____; all the intelligence in the world does not help if you are not able to manage your time.
    a) Perspicacity…Ambition
    b) Decorum…Alacrity
    c) Efficiency…Aptitude
    d) Accountability…Solicitude
    e) Wiliness…Acumen

14. Clarissa was grateful for her friend's assistance with editing down her originally _____ acceptance speech.
    a) Turgid
    b) Mellifluous
    c) Dilated
    d) Laconic
    e) Concise

15. "The party was an unmitigated disaster," Josephine said with _____, unworried about hurting anyone's feelings.
    a) Barbarity
    b) Vexation
    c) Elation
    d) Ire
    e) Candor

16. The Natural History Museum had an extensive exhibit which explained how scientists were able to learn the habits of _____ mammals from the _____ remains of their bodies.
    a) Extinct…Ossified
    b) Reserved…Mummified
    c) Omnivorous…Decayed
    d) Ambiguous…Coded
    e) Wary…Petrified

17. Erin _____ the volume of the music coming through her headphones in an effort to _____ the conversation of the men sitting behind her on the bus.
    a) Diminished…Conceal
    b) Terminated…Transcribe
    c) Maximized…Amplify
    d) Elevated…Obstruct
    e) Mitigated…Fathom

18. It is our opinion that preventing others from accessing information that could be helpful to them is _____ act.
- a) A transient
- b) An exceptionable
- c) A tractable
- d) An irascible
- e) An egalitarian

19. We ____ rejected the amendment; no argument or plea could persuade us to reverse our position.
- a) Equivocally
- b) Harmoniously
- c) Lugubriously
- d) Categorically
- e) Ambiguously

20. Even though the latest tests had _____ an outbreak as a possibility, the _____ of the epidemic continued to frighten the research team.
- a) Eliminated...Ruse
- b) Fourished...Reprieve
- c) Eradicated...Specter
- d) Delineated...Chance
- e) Subjugated...Theory

21. The author was rarely intrigued by the _____ details of detective work; rather, he explored the exciting moments of danger and suspense.
- a) Mundane
- b) Anxious
- c) Listless
- d) Copious
- e) Definitive

22. The introduction to the new edition of essays _____ the virtues of the author, who had won several literary prizes.
- a) Impugned
- b) Extolled
- c) Revamped
- d) Improvised
- e) Desecrated

23. Given the limited resources available, it would not be _____ to _____ what we have.
- a) Boorish...Appropriate
- b) Asinine...Aggregate
- c) Expedient...Squander
- d) Prudent...Inhibit
- e) Facetious...Ruin

24. The fundraising dinner at the museum was attended by a _____ group of artists, business owners, students, socialites, and publishers.
- a) Heterogeneous
- b) Contentious
- c) stimulating
- d) Prosaic
- e) Outlandish

25. Niku refused to acknowledge the _____ in her opinion against the expansion of tourism while she herself invested in the ___ chain of hotels.
- a) Duplicity...Extravagant
- b) Consistency...Growing
- c) Righteousness...Declining
- d) Hypocrisy...Burgeoning
- e) Relevance...Lucrative

Test Your Knowledge: Vocabulary – Answers

1. **b)**
Prescient: Having knowledge of things or events before they happen; having foresight.

2. **a)**
Equatorial: Typical of the regions at the earth's equator. **Impervious**: Not permitting penetration or passage.

3. **d)**
Systematizing: Making systematic; arranging in a system. **Digitized**: Converting to digital form.

4. **c)**
Pretext: Something put forward to conceal a true purpose.

5. **c)**
Abrogate: To abolish by formal or official means.

6. **e)**
Zest: An agreeable flavor imparted to something. **Undermined**: To injure or destroy something by stages.

7. **e)**
Holistically: Incorporating the principle that whole entities have an existence greater than the sum of their parts.

8. **a)**
Precise: Operating with total accuracy. **Deduced**: Arrived at a conclusion from something known; to infer.

9. **e)**
Perpetuate: To preserve from extinction. **Instruct**: To furnish with knowledge.

10. **b)**
Jovial: Characterized by a hearty, joyous humor.

11. **b)**
Adamant: Utterly unyielding in attitude or opinion despite all appeals.

12. **a)**
Consistent: Steady; even.

13. **b)**
Efficiency: The production of desired effects with minimum waste of time or effort. **Aptitude**: Inherent ability; intelligence.

14. **a)**
Turgid: Swollen; pompous.

15. e)

Candor: Openness; honesty.

16. a)

Extinct: No longer in existence. Ossified: the calcification of soft tissue into bonelike material.

17. d)

Elevated: Raised. Obstruct: block out.

18. b)

Exceptionable: Objectionable.

19. d)

Categorically: Without exceptions or conditions; absolute.

20. c)

Eradicated: Removed or destroyed utterly. **Specter**: Some object or source of terror or dread.

21. a)

Mundane: Common; ordinary; banal.

22. b)

Extolled: Praised lavishly.

23. c)

Expedient: Suitable or wise under the circumstance. **Squander**: Use wastefully.

24. a)

Heterogeneous: Different in kind, unlike; incongruous.

25. d)

Hypocrisy: Pretense of morality that one does not really possess. **Burgeoning**: Growing or developing quickly.

Chapter 3: Language – Multiple Choice

The multiple-choice writing questions include sentence improvement questions and error identification questions, both of which require an understanding of correct grammar and usage.

The following is a sample of the kind of sentence improvement questions you will encounter on the CHSPE. Carefully read and answer these questions, and then check your answers afterwards.

Paragraph A
(1) Of the two types of eclipses, the most common is the lunar eclipse, which occurs when a full moon passes through Earth's shadow. (2) The disc-shaped moon slowly disappears completely or turns a coppery red color. (3) Solar and lunar eclipses both occur from time to time.

Paragraph B
(4) During a solar eclipse, the moon passes between the Earth and Sun. (5) As the moon moves into alignment, it blocks the light from the Sun creating an eerie darkness. (6) When the moon is perfectly in position, the Sun's light is visible as a ring, or corona, around the dark disc of the moon. (7) A lunar eclipse can be viewed from anywhere on the nighttime half of Earth, a solar eclipse can only be viewed from a zone that is only about 200 miles wide and covers about one-half of a percent of Earth's total area.

1. Sentence 1: "Of the two types of eclipses, the most common is the lunar eclipse, which occurs when a full moon passes through Earth's shadow." What revision is necessary in this sentence?
   a) Change "most" to "more."
   b) Change "occurs" to "occur."
   c) Change "which" to "that."
   d) Change "Earth's" to "Earths'."
   e) No correction is necessary.

2. Sentence 2: "The disc-shaped moon slowly disappears completely or turns a coppery red color." If you rewrote sentence 2, beginning with "The disc-shaped moon slowly turns a coppery red color," the next word should be:
   a) And.
   b) But.
   c) When.
   d) Because.
   e) Or.

3. Paragraph A's effectiveness could be improved by making which revision?
   a) No revision is necessary.
   b) Move sentence 3 to the beginning of the paragraph.
   c) Remove sentence 2.
   d) Move sentence 2 to the beginning of the paragraph.
   e) Remove sentence 1.

4. Sentence 7: "A lunar eclipse can be viewed from anywhere on the nighttime half of <u>Earth, a solar eclipse</u> can only be viewed from a zone that is only about 200 miles wide and covers about one-half of a percent of Earth's total area." Select the option that indicates the best way to rewrite the underlined part of this sentence. If the original is the best way, choose option **a)**.

    a) "Earth, a solar eclipse"
    b) "Earth a solar eclipse"
    c) "Earth; a solar eclipse"
    d) "Earth, because a solar eclipse"
    e) "Earth, when a solar eclipse"

Answers:

1. a)
Use the comparative "more" when comparing only two things. Here, you comparing two types of eclipses, so "more" is correct. The other changes introduce errors.

2. e)
The clauses are joined by the conjunction "or" in the original sentence. Maintaining this conjunction maintains the original relationship between ideas.

3. b)
As sentence 3 would serve as a good topic sentence, as well as an effective lead into sentence 1, the paragraph could be improved by moving sentence 3 to the beginning.

4. c)
The two related sentences should be separated by a semicolon. The other answers introduce incorrect punctuation or an inaccurate relationship between the sentences.

BASIC REVIEW: LANGUAGE

The following pages will refresh your knowledge of basic grammatical structures, of which you must have a firm command for both the multiple choice and essay portion of the Language Section. Also review those concepts explained in the Reading Comprehension and Vocabulary Chapters of this book – particularly that of diction, word choice, and topic sentences; all will help in expanding and refining your language skills.

Nouns, Pronouns, Verbs, Adjectives, and Adverbs

Nouns

Nouns are people, places, or things. They are typically the subject of a sentence. For example, "The hospital was very clean." The noun is "hospital;" it is the "place."

Pronouns

Pronouns essentially "replace" nouns. This allows a sentence to not sound repetitive. Take the sentence: "Sam stayed home from school because Sam was not feeling well." The word "Sam" appears twice in the same sentence. Instead, you can use a pronoun and say, "Sam stayed at home because *he* did not feel well." Sounds much better, right?

Most Common Pronouns:

- I, me, mine, my.

- You, your, yours.

- He, him, his.

- She, her, hers.

- It, its.

- We, us, our, ours.

- They, them, their, theirs.

Verbs

Remember the old commercial, "Verb: It's what you do"? That sums up verbs in a nutshell! Verbs are the "action" of a sentence; verbs "do" things.

They can, however, be quite tricky. Depending on the subject of a sentence, the tense of the word (past, present, future, etc.), and whether or not they are regular or irregular, verbs have many variations.

Example: "He runs to second base." The verb is "runs." This is a "regular verb."

Example: "I am 7 years old." The verb in this case is "am." This is an "irregular verb."

As mentioned, verbs must use the correct tense – and that tense must remain the same throughout the sentence. "I was baking cookies and eat some dough." That sounded strange, didn't it? That's because the two verbs "baking" and "eat" are presented in different tenses. "Was baking" occurred in the past; "eat," on the other hand, occurs in the present. Instead, it should be "**ate** some dough."

Adjectives

Adjectives are words that describe a noun and give more information. Take the sentence: "The boy hit the ball." If you want to know more about the noun "boy," then you could use an adjective to describe it. "The **little** boy hit the ball." An adjective simply provides more information about a noun or subject in a sentence.

Adverb

For some reason, many people have a difficult time with adverbs – but don't worry! They are really quite simple. Adverbs are similar to adjectives in that they provide more information; however, they describe verbs, adjectives, and even other adverbs. They do **not** describe nouns – that's an adjective's job.

Take the sentence: "The doctor said she hired a new employee."

It would give more information to say: "The doctor said she **recently** hired a new employee." Now we know more about *how* the action was executed. Adverbs typically describe when or how something has happened, how it looks, how it feels, etc.

Good vs. Well

A very common mistake that people make concerning adverbs is the misuse of the word "good."

"Good" is an adjective – things taste good, look good, and smell good. "Good" can even be a noun – "Superman does good" – when the word is speaking about "good" vs. "evil." HOWEVER, "good" is never an adverb.

People commonly say things like, "I did really good on that test," or, "I'm good." Ugh! This is NOT the correct way to speak! In those sentences, the word "good" is being used to describe an action: how a person **did**, or how a person **is**. Therefore, the adverb "well" should be used. "I did really **well** on that test." "I'm **well**."

The correct use of "well" and "good" can make or break a person's impression of your grammar – make sure to always speak correctly!

Test Your Knowledge: Multiple Choice

For questions 1 – 10, select the best segment to replace the underlined segment of the sentence.

1. Rod cells are found in the human eye so they can absorb light to see in even dim environments.
   a) "eye, but can absorb light to see in even dim environments."
   b) "eye to see in dim environments even by absorbing light."
   c) "eye and can absorb light to see in even dim environments."
   d) "eye and are absorbing light to see in even dim environments."
   e) "eye so they can absorb light to see in even dim environments."

2. Having already finished her essay, washing the truck was the thing Maricela was ready to do.
   a) "washing the truck was the next thing Maricela did."
   b) "Maricela had another thing she was ready to do and that was washing the truck."
   c) "washing the truck Maricela was ready to do."
   d) "Maricela was ready to wash the truck."
   e) "washing the truck was the thing Maricela was ready to do."

3. The information gathered from the national census is used to determine political boundaries, inform policies, and planning transportation systems.
   a) "is used to determine political boundaries, inform policies, and plan transportation systems."
   b) "determines political boundaries and informs policies and plans transportation systems."
   c) "is determining political boundaries, informing policies, and planning transportation systems."
   d) "is used to determine political boundaries, informing policies, and planning transportation systems."
   e) "is used to determine political boundaries, inform policies, and planning transportation systems."

4. Many artists and producers disagree over how copyright laws should be applied, they have different perspectives on what best protects and encourages creativity.
   a) "should be applied since it is that they have different perspectives"
   b) "are applied with different perspectives"
   c) "should apply on differing perspectives"
   d) "are applied, because they have different perspectives"
   e) "should be applied, they have different perspectives"

5. Many consider television shows to be eroding of our nation's imaginations and attention spans.
   a) "to have eroded our nation's imaginations and attention spans."
   b) "erosion of our nation's imaginations and attention spans."
   c) "to be eroding of our national imaginations and attention spans."
   d) "to be eroding of the national imagination and attention span."
   e) "eroded our nation's imaginations and attention spans."

43

6. In the early 1960's, the Civil Rights movement in the United States <u>has swiftly grown to encompass</u> such movements as the Freedom Rides and the integration of universities.
    a) "has grown swiftly to encompass"
    b) "has swiftly grown, encompassing"
    c) "growing swiftly has encompassed"
    d) "had swiftly grown to encompass"
    e) "has swiftly grown to encompass"

7. Raul, the most knowledgeable of us all regarding physics, <u>maintain that we would be needing</u> better equipment.
    a) "maintaining that we would need"
    b) "maintains that we would be needing"
    c) "maintains that we would need"
    d) "maintain we would have needed"
    e) "maintain that we would be needing"

8. <u>Does anyone have an informed guess that they would like</u> to share before I reveal the answer?
    a) "Do anyone have an informed guess that they would like"
    b) "Is anyone having an informed guess that they would like"
    c) "Does anyone have an informed guess that they have wanting"
    d) "Anyone with an informed guess would like"
    e) "Does anyone have an informed guess that they would like"

9. <u>The meals at this restaurant have so much more salt in them than the restaurant we went to last week.</u>
    a) "The meals at this restaurant have so much more salt in them than that other restaurant."
    b) "The meals at this restaurant are so much saltier than the restaurant we went to last week."
    c) "The meals at this restaurant have much more salt in them than the restaurant we went to last week."
    d) "The meals at this restaurant have so much more salt in them than those at the restaurant we went to last week."
    e) "The meals at this restaurant have so much more salt in them than the restaurant we went to last week."

10. The Bernina Range <u>runs along eastern Switzerland and is considered to be a part of the</u> Central Eastern Alps.
    a) "is running along eastern Switzerland and is considered to be a part of the"
    b) "runs along eastern Switzerland and is considered part of"
    c) "run along eastern Switzerland, consider to be a part of the"
    d) "run along eastern Switzerland and is considered to be a part of the"
    e) "runs along eastern Switzerland and is considered to be a part of the"

For the following questions, select which of the underlined selections are incorrect within the sentence.

11. When cooking with hot <u>oil, it is prudent</u> for <u>one to wear</u> long sleeves so that want the oil does not <u>splatter onto</u> your arms and burn <u>them</u>.
    a) "oil, it is prudent"
    b) "one to wear"
    c) "splatter onto"
    d) "them."
    e) No error.

12. <u>Jordan and I</u> practiced our show <u>over and over;</u> we <u>would have</u> only twenty minutes to play, and we wanted to make sure <u>to play</u> our best songs.
    a) "Jordan and I"
    b) "over and over;"
    c) "would have"
    d) "to play"
    e) No error.

13. Aliyah asked <u>Timothy and I</u> to help her run the student <u>election;</u> so this week <u>we are hanging</u> posters, printing the ballots, <u>and editing speeches</u>.
    a) "Timothy and I"
    b) "election"
    c) "we are hanging"
    d) "and editing speeches."
    e) No error.

14. The difficulty with navigating <u>subway systems</u> <u>are compounded</u> <u>when some</u> stations are closed for <u>repair</u>.
    a) "subway systems"
    b) "are compounded"
    c) "when some"
    d) "repair."
    e) No error.

15. We <u>were given</u> explicit instructions for how to deal with <u>this exact</u> situation: we are to <u>immediately halt</u> production <u>and be contacting</u> the supervisor.
    a) "were given"
    b) "this exact"
    c) "to immediately halt"
    d) "and be contacting"
    e) No error.

16. The way the <u>shadows play</u> across the leaves <u>provide the artist</u> with <u>innumerable</u> challenges in painting the <u>twilit landscape</u>.
    a) "shadows play"
    b) "provide the artist"
    c) "innumerable"
    d) "the twilit landscape"
    e) No error.

17. <u>Along the banks</u> of the Colorado River <u>grow many different kinds</u> of bushes and trees <u>which serve</u> as habitats for the deer mice, raccoons, jackrabbits, and toads <u>that live there</u>.
    a) "Along the banks"
    b) "grow many different kinds"
    c) "which serve"
    d) "that live there"
    e) No error.

18. Gerald <u>slung his arm</u> about me <u>very</u> <u>familiar, although</u> we had <u>only met hours ago</u>.
    a) "slung his arm"
    b) "very"
    c) "familiar, although"
    d) "only met hours ago"
    e) No error.

19. After hiking <u>all afternoon</u> in the rocky desert, <u>we had</u> a desperate <u>need of</u> water bottles and <u>long, soothing showers</u>.
    a) "all afternoon"
    b) "we had"
    c) "need of"
    d) "long, soothing showers"
    e) No error.

20. It took nearly <u>half an hour</u> to dish out the meals to the large group. First, we had to <u>give everyone food</u>, and then we had to make sure <u>that everyone got</u> <u>their beverage</u> as well.
    a) "half an hour"
    b) "give everyone food"
    c) "that everyone got"
    d) "their beverage"
    e) No error.

21. When considering <u>what kind of</u> car to purchase, it is important to <u>factor in hidden costs</u> such as how much gas <u>the car consumed</u> and how expensive <u>maintenance will be</u>.
    a) "what kind of"
    b) factor in hidden costs"
    c) "the car consumed
    d) "maintenance will be"
    e) No error.

22. Just before <u>the guests arrived</u> Sarah realized that <u>we were going</u> to run out of paper plates, so <u>her and David</u> went to the store to buy <u>some</u>.
- a) "the guests arrived"
- b) "we were going"
- c) "her and David"
- d) "some"
- e) No error.

23. <u>Regardless by</u> how much one <u>likes or appreciates</u> a gift, it is <u>absolutely necessary</u> to thank the giver in person, by telephone, <u>or even with</u> a card.
- a) "Regardless by"
- b) "likes or appreciates"
- c) "absolutely necessary"
- d) "or even with"
- e) No error.

24. Even though Alaina <u>was generally cautious</u> when it came to daring physical feats, she was excited <u>to try</u> spelunking for the first time; <u>she'd heard</u> that <u>the caves were</u> breathtaking.
- a) "was generally cautious"
- b) "to try"
- c) "she'd heard"
- d) "the caves were"
- e) No error.

25. The <u>borders of</u> Rasco County <u>is comprised</u> of the river to the north <u>and east</u> and interstates <u>along the south</u> and the west.
- a) "borders of"
- b) "is comprised"
- c) "and east"
- d) "along the south"
- e) No error.

26. Each <u>applicant for</u> the open time slot <u>was asked</u> to give <u>his opinion on</u> the best way to improve the radio <u>station's programming</u>.
- a) "applicant for"
- b) "was asked"
- c) "his opinion on"
- d) "station's programming"
- e) No error.

27. There <u>will likely never</u> be a general <u>consensus on</u> which <u>is best</u>: the sunrise <u>or</u> the sunset.
- a) "will likely never"
- b) "consensus on"
- c) "is best'
- d) "or"
- e) No error.

28. The storm drew <u>menacing</u> near the town <u>where</u> citizens <u>had been</u> warned to move down to <u>their</u> cellars.
   a) "menacing"
   b) "where"
   c) "had been"
   d) "their"
   e) No error .

29. There are some difficulties inherent <u>for moving</u> across the country. <u>One must</u> secure housing <u>remotely</u> and <u>transport</u> belongings great distances.
   a) "for moving"
   b) "One must"
   c) "remotely"
   d) "transport"
   e) No error.

30. <u>When driving</u> on a <u>major</u> road, <u>to have gone</u> the speed limit <u>is prudent</u>.
   a) "When driving"
   b) "major"
   c) "to have gone"
   d) "is prudent"
   e) No error.

31. Salvador <u>and me</u>, <u>who take</u> Spanish class <u>together</u>, often study in the library <u>prior to</u> exams.
   a) "and me"
   b) "who take"
   c) "together"
   d) "prior to"
   e) No error.

32. <u>Because of</u> the stringent law <u>enacted in</u> the state, legislators <u>must be careful</u> to review <u>policies</u>.
   a) "Because of"
   b) "enacted in"
   c) "must be careful"
   d) "policies"
   e) No error.

33. <u>If the candidate</u> the company <u>had endorsed</u> were <u>to win</u>, the CEO <u>is very</u> pleased.
   a) "If the candidate"
   b) "had endorsed"
   c) "to win"
   d) "is very"
   e) No error.

34. <u>Even though</u> we <u>already understood</u> the solution, the tutor <u>insisted on</u> explaining the steps again to Sara <u>and I</u>.

    a) "Even though"
    b) "already understood"
    c) "insisted on"
    d) "and I"
    e) No error.

35. It is essential to <u>applying</u> the <u>criteria</u> uniformly across all of the candidates <u>in order to</u> judge the contest <u>fairly</u>.

    a) "applying"
    b) "criteria"
    c) "in order to"
    d) "fairly"
    e) No error.

For the following questions, rewrite the sentence in your mind using the provided start of the sentence, then choose the correct answer for what should follow.

36. Ice, which expands when frozen, will take up more space within the container holding it.

    Rewrite, beginning with: <u>Expanding when frozen,</u>

    The next words will be:

    a) "the container holding it"
    b) "take up more space"
    c) "space is taken"
    d) "ice will take up"
    e) "holding it"

37. Michael, John, and Jerry all enjoy playing football on warm summer mornings if they can find a team to join them.

    Rewrite, beginning with: <u>On warm summer mornings,</u>

    The next words will be:

    a) "Michael, John, and Jerry"
    b) "playing football"
    c) "enjoy the playing of"
    d) "finding a team to join them"
    e) "the team that joins them"

38. The office party was a success, everyone agreed happily, especially because of the good food.
Rewrite, beginning with: <u>Especially because of the good food,</u>

The next words will be:

a) "agreed"
b) "happily agreed"
c) "a success"
d) "the office"
e) "everyone agreed"

39. Dogs are faithful companions, and can be great addition to any family; but not all dogs are well-suited for hunting and outdoor activities.

Rewrite, beginning with: <u>A great addition to any family,</u>

The next words will be:

a) "All dogs"
b) "dogs are faithful"
c) "companions are"
d) "my dog is black"
e) "hunting and outdoor"

40. Jill was excited after finally learning how to ride a bike.

Rewrite, beginning with: <u>Finally learning how to ride a bike</u>

The next words will be:

a) "was excited"
b) "afterwards Jill"
c) "she was riding"
d) "excited Jill"
e) "finally excited"

Test Your Knowledge: Multiple Choice – Answers

1. c)
Wordiness and precision.

2. d)
Misplaced modifier and wordiness.

3. a)
Parallelism in listing, subject/verb agreement.

4. d)
Word usage.

5. a)
Verb tense.

6. d)
Verb tense.

7. c)
Subject/verb agreement and gerund use.

8. e)
No error.

9. d)
Imprecise comparisons.

10. e)
No error.

11. b)
"One" and "you" cannot both be used as forms of address in the same sentence.

12. e)
No error.

13. a)
Subject/object pronoun use ("Timothy and me").

14. b)
Subject/verb agreement ("Difficulty is compounded")

15. d)
Parallelism ("and contact")

16. b)
Subject/verb agreement ("The way…provides the artist").

17. e)
No error.

18. c)
Adjective/adverb use ("familiarly although").

19. c)
Proper idiomatic usage ("need for").

20. d)
Subject/verb agreement ("everyone got his or her beverage").

21. c)
Verb tense ("the car will consume").

22. c)
Subject/object pronoun ("David and she went to the store").

23. a)
Proper idiomatic usage ("Regardless of").

24. e)
No error.

25. b)
Subject/verb agreement ("are comprised").

26. c)
Pronoun agreement ("his or her opinion").

27. c)
Superlative use ("is better," since only two things are being compared).

28. a)
Adjective/adverb use ("menacingly").

29. a)
Idiomatic usage ("inherent in/to moving").

30. c)
Verb tense ("going").

31. a)
Subject/object pronoun use ("and I").

32. e)
No error.

33. d)
Verb tense/subjunctive ("would be very").

34. d)
Subject/object pronoun use ("and me").

35. a)
Verb tense ("apply").

36. d)

37. a)

38. e)

39. b)

40. d)

Chapter 4: Language – Essay

Your essay will have the potential for a score of 1 to 5, with 5 being the highest.

- **Score of 4 – 5**: This is a well-written essay that addresses the topic clearly and coherently; is free of errors; has a well-supported argument that includes additional information; incorporates an easy-to-read format; and uses accurate word choice.

- **Score of 3**: This is an essay that might have a few minor errors in syntax or punctuation, but those do not detract from the readers' ability to understand the meaning. The essay presents a reasonably clear argument, although supporting arguments could have been better.

- **Score of 2**: This is an essay that initially addresses the topic, but quickly loses focus and confuses the reader. Word choice is poor, and the essay includes multiple errors which are distracting. Supporting arguments are very weak and do not relate well to the topic.

- **Score of 1**: An essay scoring a 1 generally does not address the topic at all, immediately losing focus and clarity. It contains serious errors which are not only distracting, but also cause confusion for the reader. These essays either have a lack of supporting arguments, or the supporting arguments are irrelevant to the topic.

An Effective Essay Demonstrates:

1. Insightful and effective development of a point-of-view on the issue.

2. Critical thinking skills. For example: Two oppositions are given; instead of siding with one, you provide examples in which both would be appropriate.

3. Organization. It is clearly focused and displays a smooth progression of ideas.

4. Supportive information. If a statement is made, it is followed by examples, reasons, or other supporting evidence.

5. Skillful use of varied, accurate, and apt vocabulary.

6. Sentence variety. (Not every sentence follows a "subject-verb" pattern. Mix it up!)

7. Proper grammar and spelling.

Things to Keep in Mind While Writing Your Essay

- **Rhetorical Force**: This factor judges how coherently the writer composes their essay. How clear is the idea or argument that is being presented?

- **Organization**: The writing must have a logical order, so that the reader can easily follow along and understand the main points being made.

- **Support and Development**: The use and quality of supporting arguments and information. Essays should not be vague.

- **Usage**: Essays should demonstrate a competent command of word choice, showing both accuracy and quality in the words used.

- **Structure and Convention**: Essays should be free of errors, including: spelling, punctuation, capitalization, sentence structure, etc.

- **Appropriateness**: Essays should be written in a style appropriate for the topic; they should also contain material appropriate for both the topic and the audience.

- **Timing**: You will only have about 30 – 35 minutes within which to write your essay. Pace yourself; and practice, practice, practice!

In this chapter, we will provide a sample CHSPE essay prompt, followed by four short sample responses. The four sample responses each display different qualities of work; an explanation will follow each sample, explaining what score it would have earned and why.

Essay Examples and Evaluations

Prompt:
Research tells us that what children learn in their earliest years is very important to their future success in school. Because of this, public schools all over the country are starting to offer Pre-Kindergarten classes.

What are the benefits of starting school early? What are some of the problems you see in sending four-year-olds to school?

Write a composition in which you weigh the pros and cons of public school education for Pre-Kindergartners. Give reasons and specific examples to support your opinion. There is no specific word limit for your composition, but it should be long enough to give a clear and complete presentation of your ideas.

Sample Score 4+ Essay

Today, more and more four-year-olds are joining their big brothers and sisters on the school bus and going to Pre-Kindergarten. Although the benefits of starting school early are clear, it is also clear that Pre-K is not for every child.

The students who are successful in Pre-K are ahead when they start kindergarten. Pre-K teaches them to play well with others. Even though it does not teach skills like reading and writing, it does help to prepare students for "real" school. Pre-K students sing songs, dance, paint and draw, climb and run. They learn to share and to follow directions. They tell stories and answer questions, and as they do, they add new words to their vocabularies. Pre-K can also give students experiences they might not get at home. They might take trips to the zoo or the farm, have visits from musicians or scientists, and so on. These experiences help the students better understand the world.

There are, however, some real differences among children of this age. Some four-year-olds are just not ready for the structure of school life. Some have a hard time leaving home, even for only three or four hours a day. Other children may already be getting a great preschool education at home or in daycare.

While you weigh the advantages and disadvantages of Pre-K, it is safe to say that each child is different. For some children, it is a wonderful introduction to the world of school. But others may not or should not be forced to attend Pre-K.

Evaluation of Sample Score 4 Essay

This paper is clearly organized and has stated a definite point of view. The paper opens with an introduction and closes with a conclusion. The introduction and conclusion combine an expression of the writer's opinion. Connections to the writer's opinion are made throughout the paper.

Sample Score 3 Essay

Just like everything in life, there are pros and cons to early childhood education. Pre-K classes work for many children, but they aren't for everyone. The plusses of Pre-K are obvious. Pre-K children learn many skills that will help them in kindergarten and later on. Probably the most important thing they learn is how to follow directions. This is a skill they will need at all stages of their life.

Other plusses include simple tasks like cutting, coloring in the lines, and learning capital letters. Many children don't get these skills at home. They need Pre-K to prepare them for kindergarten.

The minuses of Pre-K are not as obvious, but they are real. Children at this young age need the comfort of home. They need to spend time with parents, not strangers. They need that security. If parents are able to, they can give children the background they need to do well in school.

Other minuses include the fact that a lot of four year-old children can't handle school. They don't have the maturaty to sit still, pay attention, or share with others. Given another year, they may mature enough to do just fine in school. Sometimes it's better just to wait.

So there are definitely good things about Pre-K programs in our public schools, and I would definitely want to see one in our local schools. However, I think parents should decide whether their children are ready for a Pre-K education or not.

Evaluation of Sample Score 3 Essay

This paper has an identifiable organization plan, with pros and cons listed in order. The development is easy to understand, if not somewhat simplistic. The language of the paper is uneven, with some vague turns of phrase: "Just like everything in life," "definitely some good things." The word "maturity" is also misspelled. However, the essay is clear and controlled, and generally follows written conventions. If the writer had included more developed and explicit examples and used more varied words, this paper might have earned a higher score.

Sample Score 2 Essay

Is early childhood education a good idea? It depends on the child you're talking about. Some children probally need more education in the early years and need something to do to keep out of trouble. Like if there isnt any good nursry school or day care around it could be very good to have Pre-Kindergarten at the school so those children could have a good start on life. A lot of skills could be learned in Pre-Kindergarten, for example they could learn to write their name, cut paper, do art, etc.

Of course theres some kids who wouldnt do well, acting out and so on, so they might do better staying home than going to Pre-Kindergarten, because they just arent ready for school, and maybe wouldn't even be ready for kindergarten the next year either. Some kids just act younger than others or are too baby-ish for school.

So I would suport Pre-Kindergarten in our schools, it seems like a good idea to have someplace for those kids to go. Even if some kids wouldnt do well I think enough kids would do well, and it would make a diference in their grades as they got older. All those skills that they learned would help them in the future. If we did have Pre-Kindergarten it would help their working parents too, knowing their kids were someplace safe and learning importent things for life.

Evaluation of Sample Score 2 Essay

Although the writer of this paper has some good points to make, a lack of language skills, considerable misspellings, and a certain disconnectedness of thought keep the paper from scoring high. The paper begins with a vague introduction of the topic and ends with a paragraph that expresses the author's opinion, but the rest of the paper is disorganized. The reasons given do not always have examples to support them, and the examples that are given are weak.

Sample Score 1 Essay

What are benefits? What are some of problems with sending four-year-olds to school? Well, for one problem, its hard to see how little kids would do with all those big kids around at the school. They might get bullyed or lern bad habits, so I wouldnt want my four year old around those big kids on the bus and so on. Its hard to see how that could be good for a four year old. In our area we do have Pre-Kindergarten at our school but you dont have to go there a lot of kids in the program, I think about 50 or more, you see them a lot on the play ground mostly all you see them do is play around so its hard to see how that could be too usefull. They could play around at home just as easy. A reason for not doing Pre-Kindergarten is then what do you learn in Kindergarten. Why go do the same thing two years when you could just do one year when your a little bit bigger (older). I wonder do the people who want Pre-Kindergarten just want there kids out of the house or a baby sitter for there kids. Its hard to see why do we have to pay for that. I dont even know if Kindergarten is so usefull anyway, not like first grade where you actially learn something. So I would say theres lots of problems with Pre-Kindergarten.

Evaluation of Sample Score 1 Essay

This paper barely responds to the prompt. It gives reasons not to support Pre-K instruction, but it does not present any benefits of starting school early. The writer repeats certain phrases ("It's hard to see") to no real effect, and the faulty spelling, grammar, and punctuation significantly impede understanding. Several sentences wander off the topic entirely ("there a lot of kids in the program, I think about 50 or more, you see them a lot on the playground.", "I dont even know if Kindergarten is so usefull anyway, not like first grade where you actially learn something."). Instead of opening with an introduction, the writer simply lifts phrases from the prompt. The conclusion states the writer's opinion, but the reasons behind it are illogical and vague. Rather than organizing the essay in paragraph form, the writer has written a single, run-on paragraph. The lack of organization, weak language skills, and failure to address the prompt earn this essay a 1.

Test Your Knowledge: Essay

Prompt One

Provided below is an excerpt and a question. Use the excerpt to prompt your thinking, and then plan and write an essay in 35 minutes by answering the question from your perspective. Be sure to provide evidence.

- *General George S. Patton Jr. is quoted as having said, "No good decision was ever made in a swivel chair."*

Is it necessary to be directly in a situation in order to best understand what must be done?

Prompt Two

Provided below is an excerpt and a question. Use the excerpt to prompt your thinking, and then plan and write an essay in 35 minutes by answering the question from your perspective. Be sure to provide evidence.

- *In The Dispossessed, published in 1974, groundbreaking science fiction author Ursula K. LeGuin wrote, "You can't crush ideas by suppressing them. You can only crush them by ignoring them."*

Is it possible to get rid of an idea?

Prompt Three

Provided below is an excerpt and a question. Use the excerpt to prompt your thinking, and then plan and write an essay in 35 minutes by answering the question from your perspective. Be sure to provide evidence.

- *"The paradox of education is precisely this -- that as one begins to become conscious one begins to examine the society in which he is being educated." James Baldwin (1924-1987), American novelist, poet, and social critic*

Does a successful education require the examination of one's own society?

Test Your Knowledge: Essay – Answers

The following pages hold sample scored essays for topics one, two, and three. These are just examples - there are many ways that CHSPE essays can be scored high or low. Look for: reasoning, examples, word usage, coherency, and detail. There are no "right" answers on the CHSPE essay; the most important factor is that the argument be well developed.

Essays for Prompt One

Is it necessary to be directly in a situation to best understand what must be done?

Score of 4:

General George Patton was speaking of war when he noted that "no good decision was ever made in a swivel chair;" however, that observation applies to situations beyond battle. While a big-picture perspective is useful in analyzing situations and deciding how to act, an on-the-ground outlook is essential. In matters of politics, and technology, to name two, the best-laid plans usually have to be changed to respond to changing circumstances.

One example which illustrates the necessity of on-the-ground action is the famous space flight of Apollo 13. Before launch, all plans were worked out to get the manned mission to the moon and back. However, due to a fluke set of circumstances – an oxygen tank explosion and the resulting technical problems – the plans had to change. The successful return of Apollo 13 and the survival of its crew would not have been possible without the quick thinking of the men on board. They first noticed the incident, well before the technical crew in Houston would have detected it from Earth. While the work of the technical crew was of course key as well, without the astronauts on board the ship to implement an emergency plan, the mission would surely have been lost.

Just as there are often unforeseen circumstances when implementing technology, politics can also be unpredictable. For example, the Cuban Missile Crisis in 1962 required immediate, on-the-ground decision making by the leaders of the United States. Prior to the Cold War standoff, President Kennedy and his advisors had already decided their hardline position against Soviet weapons expansion in the Western hemisphere. The Monroe Doctrine, status quo since the 1920s, held that European countries should not practice their influence in the Americas. The Soviet Union tested this line by establishing intermediate-range missiles on the island of Cuba. President Kennedy could not simply hold to the established wisdom, because the true limits had never been tested. Instead, to stave off the threat of attack, he was forced to act immediately as events unfolded to preserve the safety of American lives. The crisis unfolded minute-by-minute, with formerly confident advisors unsure of the smartest step. Eventually, after thirteen tense days, the leaders were able to reach a peaceful conclusion.

What these events of the 1960s illustrate is that the best laid plans are often rendered useless by an unfolding situation. For crises to be resolved, whether they be in war, technology, or politics; leaders must have level heads in the moment with up-to-date information. Therefore, plans established in advance by those in swivel chairs with level heads are not always the best plans to follow. History has shown us that we must be able to think on our feet as unforeseen situations unfold.

Score of 3:

It is often necessary to be directly on the ground as a situation unfolds to know what is best do to. This is because situations can be unpredictable and what you previously thought was the best course of action, is not always so. This can be seen in the unfolding events of the 1962 Cuban Missile Crisis.

The Cuban Missile Crisis happened in 1962, during the presidency of John F. Kennedy, when Nikita Khrushchev, president of the Soviet Union, developed an intermediate-range missile base on the island of Cuba, within range of the United States. Since the Monroe Doctrine in the 1920s, the United States leaders have declared that they would not tolerate this kind of aggression. However, the decisions that had been made by leaders in the past, removed from the situation, were no longer relevant. It was necessary for President Kennedy to make decisions as events unfolded.

As the Cuban Missile Crisis shows us, at turning points in history decisions have to be made as events unfold by those who are in the middle of a situation. Otherwise, we would all be acting according to what those in the past and those removed from the challenge thought was best. Following the Monroe Doctrine could have resulted in unnecessary violence.

Score of 1 – 2:

It is necessary to make decisions while in the middle of a situation, not above the situation, because there is always information that is only known to people in the middle of the situation. For example, in a war, the strategists in Washington might have an overall aim in the war, but they would be unable to know what it best to do on the ground. Situations like running out of ammunition or the enemy having an unexpected backup could change the decisions that need to be made. This was especially true before cell phones and other digital technologies made communication easier.

Essays for Prompt Two

Is it possible to get rid of an idea?

Score of 4:

The suppression of ideas has been attempted over and over throughout history by different oppressive regimes. This theme has been explored as well in literature, through such dystopian works as 1984 and Fahrenheit 451. But these histories and stories always play out the same way: eventually, the repressed idea bubbles to the surface and triumphs. Ursula K. LeGuin acknowledged this by saying that ideas can be crushed not by suppression, but by omission.

In Aldous Huxley's novel <u>Brave New World</u>, the world government maintains order not by governing people strictly and policing their ideas, but by distracting them. Consumption is the highest value of the society. When an outsider to the society comes in and questions it, he is exiled – not to punish him, but to remove his influence from society. The government of the dystopia has learned that the best way to maintain control is to keep citizens unaware of other, outside ideas. This theme resonates with a modern audience more than other, more authoritarian tales of dystopia because in our society, we are less controlled than we are influenced and persuaded.

Repressing ideas through harsh authoritarian rule has proven time and again to be ultimately fruitless. For example, in Soviet Russia during the 1920s and 1930s, Josef Stalin attempted to purge his society of all religious belief. This was done through suppression: discriminatory laws were enacted, members of the clergy were executed, and the religious citizenry were terrified. While these measures drastically crippled religious institutions, they were ineffective at completely eliminating the idea of religion. Beliefs and traditions were passed down in communities clandestinely throughout the repressive rule of Stalin. After the fall of the Soviet Union, it became clear that religion had survived all along.

We see throughout literature and history that ignoring ideas and distracting people from them is generally more effective than to attempt to stamp an idea out through means of suppression. Authoritarian rule, in fact, can do the opposite: by dramatizing and calling attention to an idea in the name of condemning it, a regime might actually strengthen that idea.

Score of 3:

We have seen different governments try to crush out ideas throughout history. However, they are never actually successful in doing so. An idea can be ignored or suppressed, but it will never really go away. This is illustrated in the survival of religion in the Soviet Union.

In Soviet Russia during the 1920s and 1930s, Josef Stalin attempted to purge the society of all religious belief. This was done through suppression: discriminatory laws, execution of the clergy, and use of terror. While this harmed religious institutions, they were ineffective at crushing the idea of religion. Beliefs and traditions were passed down in communities secretly throughout the rule of Stalin. After the fall of the Soviet Union, it became clear that religion had survived all along.

The same kind of thing happened with apartheid law in South Africa. Even though there were laws against black Africans and white Africans using the same facilities, the idea caught fire, especially because of an international outcry against the law.

We see throughout history that suppressing ideas does not crush them. Authoritarian rule, in fact, can do the opposite: by calling attention to an idea in the name of condemning it, a regime might actually strengthen that idea.

Score of 1 – 2:

It is not possible to crush out an idea by ignoring it or by suppressing it. All throughout history, whenever anyone has tried to do this, they might be temporarily successful but the idea will always survive or come back. For example in the Soviet Union religion was suppressed. People were not allowed to practice their religion. But after the government fell, religion still existed – people had held on to their ideas during the time of suppression.

Essays for Prompt Three

Does a successful education require the examination of one's own society?

Score of 4:

James Baldwin noted that education is a paradox – as one becomes educated, one starts to question the educators. This is necessarily true, because an education is not just a mastery of facts and information but also acquiring the ability to think critically and forge new connections. Progress in society comes from people who understand the thought that came before and are then able to take it one step further. This theme plays out in social activism and in science, for example.

A society's understanding of human rights is constantly evolving. For this process to continue, each generation must question the mores taught by the previous generation. This process can be seen in America in the progression of women's rights, the rights of non-whites, religious rights, and the rights of the disabled. One hundred years ago, these groups had far less constitutional protection than they do today. It takes groups of educated people with a forward-thinking understanding to advocate and press for changes to be made. To take one example, women have gone from not having the right to vote in 1912 to, one hundred years later, women beginning to run for the highest political office. This happened because people like Elizabeth Cady Stanton, a suffragist in the 1850s, and Marsha Griffiths, the Representative in Congress in the 1970s who championed for the Equal Rights Amendment, were able to take the precepts of justice and equality taught to them and take them a step further by applying them to women's rights.

This pattern of taking knowledge a step further can also be seen in the fields of science and mathematics. Sir Isaac Newton, one of the inventors of calculus, is attributed with saying he "stood on the shoulders of giants." He took the concepts well established in mathematics – geometry and algebra – and used the tools in a new way to create calculus. To do this, he had to both already understand what was known in the field but also be able to look at it critically. Without people doing this, fields like science and math would never progress.

A society that is interested in advancing, in rights, science, and every other field, must educate its citizens not to only understand the knowledge of the past but also to criticize prior thought and look at things in a new way. This is what James Baldwin meant – a truly educated person will question everything, even his or her own society, in order to progress.

Score of 3:

64

James Baldwin noted that education is a paradox – as one becomes educated, one starts to question the educators. This is true because an education is not just a mastery of facts and information but also ability to think critically and forge new connections. Progress in society comes from people who understand the thought that came before and are then able to take it one step further. One example of this is in human and political rights.

A society's understanding of human rights is constantly evolving. For this process to continue, each generation must question the mores taught by the previous generation. This process can be seen in America in the progression of women's rights, the rights of non-whites, religious rights, and the rights of the disabled. One hundred years ago, these groups had far less constitutional protection than they do today. It takes groups of educated people with a forward-thinking understanding to press for changes to be made. To take one example, women have gone from not having the right to vote in 1912 to, one hundred years later, women beginning to run for the highest political office. This happened because people like Elizabeth Cady Stanton, a suffragist in the 1850s, and Marsha Griffiths, the Representative in Congress in the 1970s who championed for the Equal Rights Amendment, were able to take the precepts of justice and equality taught to them and take them a step further by applying them to women's rights.

A society that is interested in advancing, in rights every other field, must educate its citizens not to only understand the knowledge of the past but also to criticize prior thought and look at things in a new way. This is what James Baldwin meant – a truly educated person will question everything, even his or her own society, in order to progress.

Score of 1 – 2:

James Baldwin said that education is a paradox – as one becomes educated, one starts to question the educators. He is right about this, because being educated is not just about knowing the facts. It is also about critical thinking. Without thinking critically about one's own society, then people never make progress. This was necessary for things like civil rights, they could not just accept what was taught in the schools about the rights people should have. Probably the most important part of being educated is questioning the society you live in.

Chapter 5: Mathematics

This chapter will cover the three different sections you will encounter on the CHSPE:

1. **Estimation, Measurement, Statistics**
    *   Units of length, measurement, and temperature; estimation; probability; averages; ratios; and basic arithmetic.

2. **Computation and Problem Solving**
    *   Basic operations (adding, solving, multiplication, division, etc.); algebra; and word problems.

3. **Numerical and Graphic Relationships**
    *   Understanding and interpretation of charts.

Math Concepts NOT Tested

You will not encounter any college-level concepts on the CHSPE. That means no calculus, statistics, trigonometry, etc. Don't take this to mean that the test is a breeze. If you haven't covered the courses listed above in a while, you will need to study to brush up.

The Most Common Mistakes

People make mistakes all the time – but during a test, those mistakes can make the difference between an excellent score, or one which falls below the requirements. Watch out for these common mistakes that people make on the CHSPE:

*   Answering with the wrong sign (positive / negative).

*   Mixing up the Order of Operations.

*   Misplacing a decimal.

*   Not reading the question thoroughly (and therefore providing an answer that was not asked for.)

*   Circling the wrong letter, or filling in wrong circle choice.

If you're thinking, "Those ideas are just common sense" – exactly! Most of the mistakes made on the CHSPE are simple mistakes. Regardless, they still result in a wrong answer and the loss of a potential point.

Strategies for the Mathematics Section

1. **Go Back to the Basics**: First and foremost, practice your basic skills: sign changes, order of operations, simplifying fractions, and equation manipulation. These are the skills used most on the CAHSEE, though they are applied in different contexts. Remember that when it comes right down to it, all math problems rely on the four basic skills of addition, subtraction, multiplication, and division. All that changes is the order in which they are used to solve a problem.

2. **Don't Rely on Mental Math**: Using mental math is great for eliminating answer choices, but ALWAYS WRITE IT DOWN! This cannot be stressed enough. Use whatever paper is provided; by writing and/or drawing out the problem, you are more likely to catch any mistakes. The act of writing things down forces you to organize your calculations, leading to an improvement in your CAHSEE score.

3. **The Three-Times Rule**:

   - **Step One – Read the question**: Write out the given information.

   - **Step Two – Read the question**: Set up your equation(s) and solve.

   - **Step Three – Read the question:** Ensure that your answer makes sense (is the amount too large or small; is the answer in the correct unit of measure, etc.).

4. **Make an Educated Guess**: Eliminate those answer choices which you are relatively sure are incorrect, and then guess from the remaining choices. Educated guessing is critical to increasing your score.

Math Concepts Tested on the CHSPE

You need to practice in order to score well on the test. To make the most out of your practice, use this guide to determine the areas for which you need more review. Most importantly, practice all areas under testing circumstances (a quiet area, a timed practice test, no looking up facts as you practice, etc.)

When reviewing, take your time and let your brain recall the necessary math. If you are taking the CHSPE, then you have already had course instruction in these areas. The examples given will "jog" your memory.

The next few pages will cover various math subjects (starting with the basics, but in no particular order), along with worked examples.

Percentile

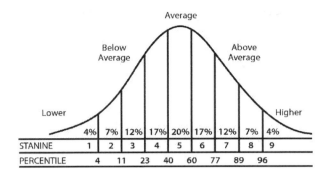

A percentile curve is simply a comparison of results relative to all other results. As you can see, if your score is a stanine of 5, you are right in the middle at the 50th percentile. This means that you did better than half of everyone else, but half did better than you. Approximately 20% of takers will fall into the stanine score range of 5.

Percentile scores do not indicate how many questions answered correctly, only how well you performed against everyone else. For example, if the score range is 90 –100, that means that everyone did very well; but those who scored a 90 are still in the stanine range of 1.

> **Example**: If you and 20% of the rest of your class scored a 95 on a test, using the chart above, would your stanine score be?

> **5** (50th Percentile)

Positive & Negative Number Rules

$(+) + (-)$	Subtract the two numbers. Solution keeps the sign of the larger number.
$(-) + (-)$	Negative number.
$(+) \times (-)$	Negative number.
$(-) \times (-)$	Positive number.
$(+) \div (-)$	Negative number.
$(-) \div (-)$	Positive number.

Greatest Common Factor (GCF)

The greatest factor divisible between two numbers.

> **Example**: The GCF of 24 and 18 is 6. 6 is the largest number, or greatest factor, that can divide both 24 and 18.

Order of Operations

PEMDAS – **P**arentheses/**E**xponents/**M**ultiply/**D**ivide/**A**dd/**S**ubtract

Perform the operations within parentheses first, and then any exponents. After those steps, perform all multiplication and division. (These are done from left to right, as they appear in the problem)

Finally, do all required addition and subtraction, also from left to right as they appear in the problem.

Examples:

1. Solve $(-(2)^2 - (4 + 7))$:
   - $(-4 - 11) = -15$.

2. Solve $((5)^2 \div 5 + 4 * 2)$:
   - $25 \div 5 + 4 * 2$.
   - $5 + 8 = 13$.

Probabilities

A probability is found by dividing the number of desired outcomes by the number of possible outcomes. (The piece divided by the whole.)

Example: What is the probability of picking a blue marble if 3 of the 15 marbles are blue?

$3/15 = 1/5$. The probability is **1 in 5** that a blue marble is picked.

Fractions

Adding and subtracting fractions requires a common denominator.

Find a common denominator for:

$$\frac{2}{3} - \frac{1}{5}.$$

$$\frac{2}{3} - \frac{1}{5} = \frac{2}{3}\left(\frac{5}{5}\right) - \frac{1}{5}\left(\frac{3}{3}\right) = \frac{10}{15} - \frac{3}{15} = \frac{7}{15}.$$

To add mixed fractions, work first the whole numbers, and then the fractions.

$$2\frac{1}{4} + 1\frac{3}{4} = 3\frac{4}{4} = 4.$$

To subtract mixed fractions, convert to single fractions by multiplying the whole number by the denominator and adding the numerator. Then work as above.

$$2\frac{1}{4} - 1\frac{3}{4} = \frac{9}{4} - \frac{7}{4} = \frac{2}{4} = \frac{1}{2}.$$

To multiply fractions, convert any mixed fractions into single fractions and multiply across; reduce to lowest terms if needed.

$$2\frac{1}{4} * 1\frac{3}{4} = \frac{9}{4} * \frac{7}{4} = \frac{63}{16} = 3\frac{15}{16}.$$

To divide fractions, convert any mixed fractions into single fractions, flip the second fraction, and then multiply across.

$$2\frac{1}{4} \div 1\frac{3}{4} = \frac{9}{4} \div \frac{7}{4} = \frac{9}{4} * \frac{4}{7} = \frac{36}{28} = 1\frac{8}{28} = \mathbf{1\frac{2}{7}}.$$

Simple Interest

Interest * Principle.

Example: If I deposit $500 into an account with an annual rate of 5%, how much will I have after 2 years?

1st year: 500 + (500*.05) = 525.

2nd year: 525 + (525*.05) = **551.25**.

Prime Factorization

Expand to prime number factors.

Example: 104 = 2 * 2 * 2 * 13.

Absolute Value

A number's absolute value is its distance from zero, not its value.

So in $|x| = a$, "x" will equal "$-a$" as well as "a."

Likewise, $|\,3\,| = 3$, and $|-3\,| = 3$.

Equations with absolute values will have two answers. Solve each absolute value possibility separately. All solutions must be checked into the original equation.

Example: Solve for x: $|4x - 5| = x + 1$

1. Equation One: $4x - 5 = -(x + 1)$.
    - $4x - 5 = -x - 1$.
    - $4x = 5$.
    - $x = \mathbf{5/4}$.

2. Equation Two: $2x - 3 = x + 1$.
    - $x = \mathbf{4}$.

Mean, Median, Mode

Mean is a math term for "average." Total all terms and divide by the number of terms.
Find the mean of 24, 27, and 18.
$24 + 27 + 18 = 69 \div 3 = \mathbf{23}$.

Median is the middle number of a given set, found after the numbers have all been put in numerical order. In the case of a set of even numbers, the middle two numbers are averaged.

What is the median of 24, 27, and 18?

18, **24**, 27.

What is the median of 24, 27, 18, and 19?

18, 19, 24, 27 (19 + 24 = 43. 43/2 = **21.5**).

Mode is the number which occurs most frequently within a given set.

What is the mode of 2, 5, 4, 4, 3, 2, 8, 9, 2, 7, 2, and 2?

The mode would be **2** because it appears the most within the set.

Percent, Part, & Whole

Part = Percent * Whole.

Percent = Part / Whole.

Whole = Part / Percent.

Example: Jim spent 30% of his paycheck at the fair. He spent $15 for a hat, $30 for a shirt, and $20 playing games. How much was his check? (Round to nearest dollar.)

Whole = 65 / .30 = **$217.00**.

Percent Change

Percent Change = Amount of Change / Original Amount * 100.

Percent Increase = (New Amount – Original Amount) / Original Amount * 100.

Percent Decrease = (Original Amount – New Amount) / Original Amount * 100.

Amount Increase (or **Decrease**) = Original Price * Percent Markup (or Markdown).

Original Price = New Price / (Whole - Percent Markdown [or Markup]).

Example: A car that was originally priced at $8300 has been reduced to $6995. What percent has it been reduced?

(8300 – 6995) / 8300 * 100 = **15.72%**.

Repeated Percent Change

Increase: Final amount = Original Amount $* (1 + \text{rate})^{\text{\# of changes}}$.

Decrease: Final Amount = Original Amount $* (1 - \text{rate})^{\text{\# of changes}}$.

> **Example:** The weight of a tube of toothpaste decreases by 3% each time it is used. If it weighed 76.5 grams when new, what is its weight in grams after 15 uses?
>
> Final amount = $76.5 * (1 - .3)^{15}$.
>
> $76.5 * (.97)^{15}$ = **48.44 grams**.

Combined Average

Weigh each average individual average before determining the sum.

> **Example**: If Cory averaged 3 hits per game during the summer and 2 hits per game during the fall and played 7 games in the summer and 8 games in the fall, what was his hit average overall?
>
> 1. Weigh each average.
>   - Summer: $3 * 7 = 21$.
>   - Fall: $2 * 8 = 16$.
>   - Sum: $21 + 16 = 47$.
>
> 2. Total number of games: $7 + 8 = 15$.
>
> 3. Calculate average: $47/15 = \sim$ **3.13 hits/game**.

You may need to work a combined average problem with a missing term.

> **Example**: Bobbie paid an average of $20 a piece for ten shirts. If five of the shirts averaged $15 each, what was the average cost of the remaining shirts?
>
> 1. Calculate sum: $10 * 20 = 200$.
>
> 2. Calculate sub-sum #1: $5 * 15 = 75$.
>
> 3. Calculate sub-sum #2: $200 - 75 = 125$.
>
> 4. Calculate average: $125 / 5 =$ **$25**.

Ratios

To solve a ratio, simply find the equivalent fraction. To distribute a whole across a ratio:

1. Total all parts.
2. Divide the whole by the total number of parts.
3. Multiply quotient by corresponding part of ratio.

Example: There are 90 voters in a room, and they are either Democrat or Republican. The ratio of Democrats to Republicans is 5:4. How many Republicans are there?

1. $5 + 4 = 9$.

2. $90 / 9 = 10$.

3. $10 * 4 = $ **40 Republicans**.

Proportions

Direct Proportions: Corresponding ratio parts change in the same direction (increase/decrease).

Indirect Proportions: Corresponding ratio parts change in opposite directions (as one part increases the other decreases).

Example: A train traveling 120 miles takes 3 hours to get to its destination. How long will it take if the train travels 180 miles?

120 mph: 180 mph is to x hours: 3 hours. (Write as fraction and cross multiply.)
- $120/3 = 180/x$.
- $540 = 120x$.
- $x = $ **4.5 hours**.

Arithmetic Sequence

Each term is equal to the previous term plus x.

Example: 2, 5, 8, 11.
- $2 + 3 = 5$; $5 + 3 = 8$ … etc.
- $x = $ **3**.

Geometric Sequence

Each term is equal to the previous term multiplied by x.

Example: 2, 4, 8, 16.
- $x = $ **2**.

Roots

Root of a Product: $\sqrt[n]{a \cdot b} = \sqrt[n]{a} \cdot \sqrt[n]{b}$.

Root of a Quotient: $\sqrt[n]{\dfrac{a}{b}} = \dfrac{\sqrt[n]{a}}{\sqrt[n]{b}}$.

Fractional Exponent: $\sqrt[n]{a^m} = a^{m/n}$.

Literal Equations

Equations with more than one variable. Solve in terms of one variable first.

Example: Solve for y: $4x + 3y = 3x + 2y$.

1. Combine like terms: $3y - 2y = 4x - 2x$.

2. Solve for y. $y = 2x$.

Linear Systems

A linear system requires the solving of two literal equations simultaneously. There are two different methods (Substitution and Addition) that can be used to solve linear systems.

Substitution Method: Solve for one variable first, and then substitute.

Example: Solve for x and y: $3y - 4 + x = 0$ and $5x + 6y = 11$.

1. Solve for one variable.
   - $3y - 4 + x = 0$.
   - $3y + x = 4$.
   - $x = 4 - 3y$.

2. Substitute into second equation, and solve.
   - $5(4 - 3y) + 6y = 11$.
   - $20 - 15y + 6y = 11$.
   - $20 - 9y = 11$.
   - $-9y = -9$.
   - $y = 1$.

3. Substitute into first equation.
   - $3(1) - 5 + x = 0$.
   - $-2 + x = 0$.
   - $x = 2$.

Addition Method: Manipulate one of the equations so that when added to the other, one variable is eliminated.

Example: Solve $2x + 4y = 16$ and $4x + 2y = 10$.

1. Manipulate one equation to eliminate a variable when added together.
   - $-2(2x + 4y = 8) = (-4x - 8y = -16)$.
   - $(-4x - 8y = -16) + (4x + 2y = 10)$.
   - $-6y = -6$.
   - $y = 1$.

2. Plug into an equation and solve for the other variable.
   - $2x + 4(1) = 16$.
   - $2x + 4 = 16$.
   - $2x = 12$.
   - $x = 6$.

The following is a typical word problem that would use a linear system to solve.

Example: Tommy has a collection of coins worth $5.20. He has 8 more nickels than quarters. How many of each does he have?

1. Set up equations.
   - Let n = nickels and q = quarters.
   - $.05n + .25q = 5.2$.
   - $n = q + 8$.

2. Substitute Equation 2 into Equation 1.
   - $.05(q + 8) + .25q = 5.2$.

3. Solve for q. You can ignore the decimal point and negative sign after this step because you are solving for number of coins.
   - $-.05(q + 8) + .25q = 5.2$.
   - $.05q + .4 + .25q = 5.2$.
   - $q = 16$.

4. Plug into the original equation.
   - $n = q + 8$.
   - $n = 24$.
   - $q = 16$.

Linear Equations

An equation for a straight line. The variable CANNOT have an exponent, square roots, cube roots, etc.

Example: $y = 2x + 1$ is a straight line, with "1" being the y-intercept, and "2" being the positive slope.

Algebraic Equations

When simplifying or solving algebraic equations, you need to be able to utilize all math rules: exponents, roots, negatives, order of operations, etc.

1. Add & Subtract: Only the coefficients of like terms.

   Example: $5xy + 7y + 2yz + 11xy - 5yz = 16xy + 7y - 3yz$.

2. Multiplication: First the coefficients then the variables.

76

Example: Monomial * Monomial. (Remember: a variable with no exponent has an implied exponent of 1.)

- $(3x^4y^2z)(2y^4z^5) = 6x^4y^6z^6$.

Example: Monomial * Polynomial.

- $(2y^2)(y^3 + 2xy^2z + 4z) = 2y^5 + 4xy^4z + 8y^2z$

Example: Binomial * Binomial.

- $(5x + 2)(3x + 3)$. Remember: FOIL (First, Outer, Inner, Last).

    First: $5x * 3x = 15x^2$.

    Outer: $5x * 3 = 15x$.

    Inner: $2 * 3x = 6x$.

    Last: $2 * 3 = 6$.

    Combine like terms: $15x^2 + 21x + 6$.

Example: Binomial * Polynomial.

- $(x + 3)(2x^2 – 5x – 2)$.

    First Term: $x(2x^2 – 5x – 2) = 2x^3 – 5x^2 – 2x$.

    Second term: $3(2x^2 – 5x – 2) = 6x^2 – 15x – 6$.

    Added Together: $2x^3 + x^2 – 17x – 6$.

Inequalities

Inequalities are solved like linear and algebraic equations, except the sign must be reversed when dividing by a negative number.

Example: $-7x + 2 < 6 – 5x$.

Step 1 – Combine like terms: $-2x < 4$.
Step 2 – Solve for x. (Reverse the sign): $x > $ **-2**.

Solving compound inequalities will give you two answers.

Example: $-4 \leq 2x – 2 \leq 6$.

Step 1 – Add 2 to each term to isolate x: $-2 \leq 2x \leq 8$.
Step 2: Divide by 2: $-1 \leq x \leq 4$.
Solution set is **[-1, 4]**.

Exponent Rules

Rule	Example
$x^0 = 1$	$5^0 = 1$
$x^1 = x$	$5^1 = 5$
$x^a \cdot x^b = x^{a+b}$	$5^2 * 5^3 = 5^5$
$(xy)^a = x^a y^a$	$(5 * 6)^2 = 5^2 * 6^2 = 25 * 36$
$(x^a)^b = x^{ab}$	$(5^2)^3 = 5^6$
$(x/y)^a = x^a/y^a$	$(10/5)^2 = 10^2/5^2 = 100/25$
$x^a/y^b = x^{a-b}$	$5^4/5^3 = 5^1 = 5$ (remember $x \neq 0$)
$x^{1/a} = \sqrt[a]{x}$	$25^{1/2} = \sqrt[2]{25} = 5$
$x^{-a} = \dfrac{1}{x^a}$	$5^{-2} = \dfrac{1}{5^2} = \dfrac{1}{25}$ (remember $x \neq 0$)
$(-x)^a$ = negative number if a is odd; positive number if a is even	

Fundamental Counting Principle

(The number of possibilities of an event happening) * (the number of possibilities of another event happening) = the total number of possibilities.

> **Example**: If you take a multiple choice test with 5 questions, with 4 answer choices for each question, how many test result possibilities are there?

> **Solution**: Question 1 has 4 choices; question 2 has 4 choices; etc.

4 * 4 * 4 * 4 * 4 (one for each question) = **1024 possible test results**.

Permutations

> The number of ways a set number of items can be arranged. Recognized by the use of a factorial ($n!$), with n being the number of items.

> If $n = 3$, then $3! = 3 * 2 * 1 = 6$. If you need to arrange n number of things but x number are alike, then $n!$ is divided by $x!$

>> **Example**: How many different arrangements can be made of the letters in the word **balance**?

>> **Solution**: There are 7 letters, so $n! = 7!$ But 2 letters are the same, so $x! = 2!$ Set up the equation:

$$\frac{7 * 6 * 5 * 4 * 3 * 2 * 1}{2 * 1} = \textbf{2540 ways}.$$

Combinations

> To calculate total number of possible combinations, use the formula: $n!/r!$ $(n-r)!$
> Where n = # of objects; and r = # of objects selected at a time.

Example: If seven people are selected in groups of three, how many different combinations are possible?

Solution:

$$\frac{7*6*5*4*3*2*1}{(3*2*1)(7-3)} = \textbf{210 possible combinations.}$$

Quadratics

Factoring: converting $ax^2 + bx + c$ to factored form. Find two numbers that are factors of c and whose sum is b.

Example: Factor $2x^2 + 12x + 18 = 0$.

1. If possible, factor out a common monomial: $2(x^2 - 6x + 9)$.

2. Find two numbers that are factors of 9; and also sum to -6: $2(x - \_)(x - \_)$.

3. Fill in the binomials. Be sure to check your answer and signs: $2(x - 3)(x - 3)$.

4. To solve, set each to $= 0$: $x - 3 = 0; \textbf{\textit{x}} = \textbf{3}$.

   If the equation cannot be factored (there are no two factors of c that sum to $= b$), the quadratic formula is used.

   $$x = \frac{-b \pm \sqrt{b^2 - 4ac}}{2a}$$

   Using the same equation from the above example: $a = 2$, $b = 12$, and $c = 18$. Plug into the formula and solve. Remember there will still be two answers due to the (+) and (-) before the radical.

Graphs and Charts

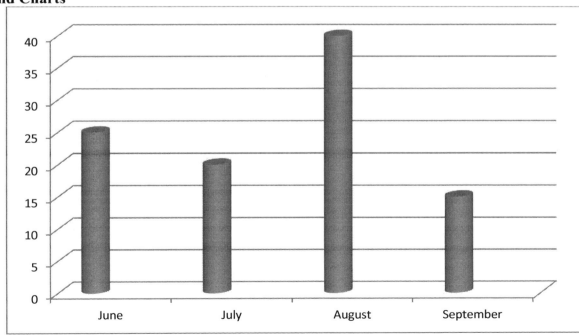

Using the above chart of ice cream sales per month, how many more sales are made in July than September? As you can see, sales in July are 20 and September sales are 15. The correct answer is therefore **5**. If you see any answer choices which are grossly incorrect – such as -10 or 20 – immediately count them out. Don't over-think graphical questions. They are typically straightforward and require only that you pay attention and don't try to answer too quickly.

Geometry

- **Obtuse Angle**: Measures greater than 90°.

- **Obtuse Triangle**: One angle measures greater than 90°.

- **Acute Angle**: Measures less than 90°.

- **Acute Triangle**: Each angle measures less than 90°.

- **Adjacent Angles**: Share a side and a vertex.

- **Complementary Angles**: Adjacent angles that sum to 90°.

- **Supplementary Angles**: Adjacent angles that sum to 180°.

- **Vertical Angles**: Angles that are opposite of each other. They are always congruent (equal in measure).

- **Isosceles Triangle**: Two sides and two angles are equivalent.

- **Equilateral Triangle**: All angles are equivalent.

- **Scalene**: No equal angles.

- **Parallel Lines**: Lines that will never intersect. Y ll X means line Y is parallel to line X.

- **Perpendicular lines**: Lines that cross, forming 90° angles.

- **Transversal Line**: A line that crosses parallel lines.

- **Bisector**: Any line that cuts a line segment, angle, or polygon exactly in half.

- **Polygon**: Any enclosed plane shape comprised of three or more connecting sides (ex. a triangle).

- **Regular Polygon**: Has all equal sides and equal angles (ex. square).

- **Arc**: A portion of a circle's edge.

- **Chord**: A line segment that connects two different points on a circle.

- **Tangent**: Something that touches a circle at only one point without crossing through it.

- **Sum of Angles**: The sum of a polygon's angles can be calculated using $(n - 1)180°$, when n = the number of sides

Triangles

The sum of angles in a triangle is 180°.
Area of a triangle = ½ * b * h, or ½bh.
Pythagoras' Theorem: $a^2 + b^2 = c^2$.

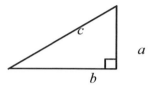

Regular Polygons

Polygon Angle Principle: $S = (n - 2)180$, where S = the sum of a polygon's interior angles with n-sides.

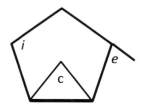

The measure of each central angle (c) is 360°/n.
The measure of each interior angle (i) is $(n - 2)180°/n$.
The measure of each exterior angle (e) is 360°/n.
To compare areas of similar polygons: $A_1/A_2 = (side_1/side_2)^2$

Trapezoids

Four-sided polygon, in which the bases (and only the bases) are parallel.

Isosceles Trapezoid: Base angles are congruent.

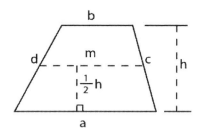

Area and Perimeter of a Trapezoid

$$m = \frac{1}{2}(a + b)$$

$$Area = \frac{1}{2}h * (a + b) = m * h$$

$$Perimeter = a + b + c + d = 2m + c + d$$

If m is the median then: $m \parallel \overline{AB}$ and $m \parallel CD$

Rhombus

Four-sided polygon, in which opposite sides are parallel and all four sides are congruent.

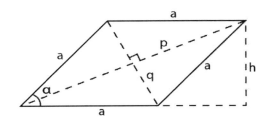

Area and Perimeter of a Rhombus

$$Perimeter = 4a$$

$$Area = a^2 \sin \alpha = a * h = \frac{1}{2}pq$$

$$4a^2 = p^2 + q^2$$

Rectangle

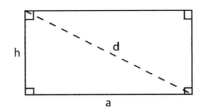

Area and Perimeter of a Rectangle

$$d = \sqrt{a^2 + h^2}$$

$$a = \sqrt{d^2 - h^2}$$

$$h = \sqrt{d^2 - a^2}$$

$$Perimeter = 2a + 2h$$

$$Area = a \cdot h$$

Square

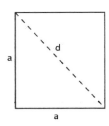

Area and Perimeter of a Square

$$d = a\sqrt{2}$$

$$Perimeter = 4a = 2d\sqrt{2}$$

$$Area = a^2 = \frac{1}{2}d^2$$

Circle

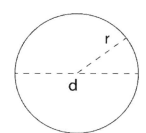

Area and Perimeter of a Circle

$$d = 2r$$

$$Perimeter = 2\pi r = \pi d$$

$$Area = \pi r^2$$

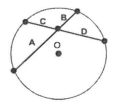

The product length of one chord equals the product length of the other, or:

AB=CD

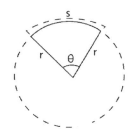

Area and Perimeter of the Sector of a Circle

$$\alpha = \frac{\theta\pi}{180} \ (rad)$$

$$s = r\alpha$$

$$Perimeter = 2r + s$$

$$Area = \frac{1}{2}\theta \, r^2 \ (radians) \ or \ \frac{n}{360}\pi r^2$$

$$length \ (l) \ of \ an \ arc \ \ l = \frac{\pi n r}{180} \ or \ \frac{n}{360} 2\pi r$$

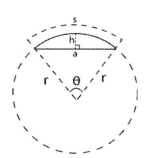

Area and Perimeter of the Segment of a Circle

$$\alpha = \frac{\theta\pi}{180} \ (rad)$$

$$a = 2\sqrt{2hr - h^2}$$

$$a^2 = 2r^2 - 2r^2 cos\theta$$

$$s = r\alpha$$

$$h = r - \frac{1}{2}\sqrt{4r^2 - a^2}$$

$$Perimeter = a + s$$

$$Area = \frac{1}{2}[sr - a(r - h)]$$

Cube

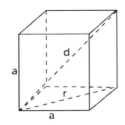

Area and Volume of a Cube

$$r = a\sqrt{2}$$

$$d = a\sqrt{3}$$

$$Area = 6a^2$$

$$Volume = a^3$$

Cuboid

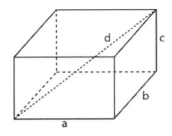

Area and Volume of a Cuboid

$$d = \sqrt{a^2 + b^2 + c^2}$$

$$A = 2(ab + ac + bc)$$

$$V = abc$$

Pyramid

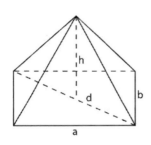

Area and Volume of a Pyramid

$$A_{lateral} = a\sqrt{h^2 + \left(\frac{b}{2}\right)^2} + b\sqrt{h^2 + \left(\frac{a}{2}\right)^2}$$

$$d = \sqrt{a^2 + b^2}$$

$$A_{base} = ab$$

$$A_{total} = A_{lateral} + A_{base}$$

$$V = \frac{1}{3}abh$$

Cylinder

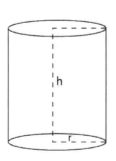

Area and Volume of a Cylinder

$$d = 2r$$

$$A_{surface} = 2\pi rh$$

$$A_{base} = 2\pi r^2$$

$$Area = A_{surface} + A_{base}$$

$$= 2\pi r\,(h + r)$$

$$Volume = \pi r^2 h$$

Cone

Area and Volume of a Cone

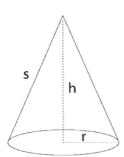

$$d = 2r$$

$$A_{surface} = \pi r s$$

$$A_{base} = \pi r^2$$

$$Area = A_{surface} + A_{base}$$

$$= 2\pi r \left(h + r \right)$$

$$Volume = \frac{1}{3} \pi r^2 h$$

Sphere

Area and Volume of a Sphere

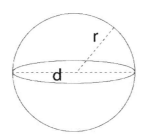

$$d = 2r$$

$$A_{surface} = 4\pi r^2$$

$$Volume = \frac{4}{3} \pi r^3$$

Test Your Knowledge: Mathematics – Question Bank

Test Your Knowledge: Percent/Part/Whole, Percent Change

1. In a class of 42 students, 18 are boys. Two girls get transferred to another school. What percent of students remaining are girls?
   a) 14%.
   b) 16%.
   c) 52.4%.
   d) 60%.
   e) None of the above.

2. A payroll check is issued for $500.00. If 20% goes to bills, 30% of the remainder goes to pay entertainment expenses, and 10% of what is left is placed in a retirement account, then approximately how much is remaining?
   a) $150.
   b) $250.
   c) $170.
   d) $350.
   e) $180.

3. A painting by Van Gogh increased in value by 80% from year 1995 to year 2000. If in year 2000, the painting is worth $7200, what was its value in 1995?
   a) $1500.
   b) $2500.
   c) $3000.
   d) $4000.
   e) $5000.

4. "Dresses and Ties" sells a particular dress for $60 dollars. But, they decide to discount the price of that dress by 25%. How much does the dress cost now?
   a) $55.
   b) $43.
   c) $45.
   d) $48.
   e) $65.

5. A sweater goes on sale for 30% off. If the original price was $70, what is the discounted price?
   a) $48.
   b) $49.
   c) $51.
   d) $65.
   e) $52.

6. If the value of a car depreciates by 60% over ten years, and its value in the year 2000 is $2500, what was its value in the year 1990?
   a) $6000.
   b) $6230.
   c) $6250.
   d) $6500.
   e) $6600.

7. If an account is opened with a starting balance of $500, what is the amount in the account after 3 years if the account pays compound interest of 5%?
   a) $560.80.
   b) $578.81.
   c) $564.50.
   d) $655.10.
   e) $660.00.

8. A piece of memorabilia depreciates by 1% every year. If the value of the memorabilia is $75000, what will it be 2 years from now? Give the answer as a whole number.
   a) $74149.
   b) $74150.
   c) $73151.
   d) $71662.
   e) $73507.

9. A dress is marked down by 20% in an effort to boost sales for one week. After that week, the price of the dress is brought back to the original value. What percent did the price of the dress have to be increased from its discounted price?
   a) 20%.
   b) 25%.
   c) 120%.
   d) 125%.
   e) 15%.

10. A car dealer increases the price of a car by 30%, but then discounts it by 30%. What is the relationship between the final price and the original price?
   a) $.91x : x$.
   b) $.98x : x$.
   c) 1:1.
   d) $.88x : x$.
   e) $.75x : x$.

Test Your Knowledge: Percent/Part/Whole, Percent – Answers

1. **e)**
   The entire class has 42 students, 18 of which are boys, meaning 42 - 18 = 24 is the number of girls. Out of these 24 girls, 2 leave; so 22 girls are left. The total number of students is now 42 - 2 = 40.

   22/40 * 100 = 55%.

   Reminder: If you forget to subtract 2 from the total number of students, you will end up with 60% as the answer. Sometimes you may calculate an answer that has been given as a choice; it can still be incorrect. Always check your answer.

2. **b)**
   If out of the entire paycheck, 20% is first taken out, then the remainder is 80%. Of this remainder, if 30% is used for entertainment, then (.8 - .80 * .30) = .560 is left. If 10% is put into a retirement account, then (.56 - .56 * .1) = .504 is remaining. So out of $500, the part that remains is 50%, which is $252.

3. **d)**
   In 2005, the value was 1.8 times its value in 1995. So $1.8x = 7200 \rightarrow x = 4000$.

4. **c)**
   60 * (100 - 25)/100 $\rightarrow$ 60 * .75 = 45.

5. **b)**
   New price = original price * (1 – discount) $\rightarrow$ new price = 70(1-.3) = 49.

6. **c)**
   $Value_{2000}$ = Original price * (1-.6) $\rightarrow$ 2500 = .4P = 2500 $\rightarrow$ P = 6250.

7. **b)**
   Amount = $P(1 + r)^t$ = 500 * 1.05^3 = $578.81.

8. **e)**
   Final value = 75000$(1 - .1)^2$ = 73507.

9. **b)**
   If the original price of the dress was x, then the discounted price would be $0.8x$. To increase the price from $.8x$ to x, the percent increase would be $(x - .8x)/.8x * 100 = 25\%$.

10. **a)**
    Let the original price of the car be x. After the 30% increase, the price is $1.3x$.

    After discounting the increased price by 30%, it now is $.7 * 1.3x = .91x$. Therefore, the ratio of the final price to the original price = $.91x : x$.

Test Your Knowledge: Mean, Median, Mode

1. If test A is taken 5 times with an average result of 21, and test B is taken 13 times with an average result of 23, what is the combined average?
    a) 22.24.
    b) 22.22.
    c) 22.00.
    d) 22.44.
    e) 24.22.

2. A set of data has 12 entries. The average of the first 6 entries is 12, the average of the next two entries is 20, and the average of the remaining entries is 4. What is the average of the entire data set?
    a) 10.
    b) 10.67.
    c) 11.
    d) 12.67.
    e) 10.5.

3. What is the average score of 8 tests where the score for 3 tests is 55, the score for two tests is 35, and the remaining tests have scores of 70?
    a) 50.3.
    b) 52.5.
    c) 55.1.
    d) 56.0.
    e) 55.6.

4. The temperatures over a week are recorded as follows:

Day	High	Low
Monday	80	45
Tuesday	95	34
Wednesday	78	47
Thursday	79	55
Friday	94	35
Saturday	67	46
Sunday	76	54

What is the approximate average high temperature and average low temperature during the week?
    a) 90, 50.
    b) 80, 40.
    c) 81, 45.
    d) 82, 46.
    e) 81, 47.

5. Twelve teams competed in a mathematics test. The scores recorded for each team are: 29, 30, 28, 27, 35, 43, 45, 50, 46, 37, 44, and 41. What is the median score?
    a) 37.
    b) 41.
    c) 39.
    d) 44.
    e) 45.

6. A class of 10 students scores 90, 78, 45, 98, 84, 79, 66, 87, 78, and 94. What is the mean score? What is the median score? What is the mode?
    a) 69.9, 81.5, 78.
    b) 79.9, 80, 78.
    c) 79.9, 87, 76.
    d) Not enough information given.
    e) None of the above.

7. A shop sells 3 kinds of t-shirts: one design sells for $4.50, the second for $13.25, and the third for $15.50. If the shop sold 8 shirts of the first design, 12 shirts of the second design, and 4 shirts of the third design, what was the average selling price of the shirts?
    a) $10.71.
    b) $10.25.
    c) $14.55.
    d) $12.55.
    e) $5.80.

Test Your Knowledge: Mean, Median, Mode – Answers

1. **d)**
   If test A avg = 21 for 5 tests, then sum of test A results = 21 * 5 = 105.
   If test B avg = 23 for 13 tests, then sum of test B results = 23 * 13 = 299.
   So total result = 299 + 105 = 404.
   Average of all tests = 404/(5 + 13) = 404/18 = 22.44.

2. **b)**
   The average of the first 6 points is 12 → $s_1/6 = 12$ → $s_1 = 72$; s_1 is the sum of the first 6 points.

   The average of the next 2 points is 20 → $s_2/2 = 20$ → $s_2 = 40$; s_2 is the sum of the next 2 points.

   The average of the remaining 4 points is 4 → $s_3/4 = 4$ → $s_3 = 16$; s_3 is the sum of the last 4 points.

   The sum of all the data points = 72 + 40 + 16 = 128.

   The average = 128/12 = 10.67.

3. **e)**
   Average = (3 * 55 + 2 * 35 + 3 * 70)/8 → Average = 55.625.

4. **c)**
   Average of high s = (80 + 95 + 78 + 79 + 94 + 67 + 76)/7 = 81.29.

   Average of low s = (45 + 34 + 47 + 55 + 35 + 46 + 54)/7 = 45.14.

5. **c)**
   To find the median, we first have to put the list in order:

   27, 28, 29, 30, 35, 37, 41, 43, 44, 45, 46, 50.

   The middle two scores are 37 and 41, and their average is 39.

6. **e) None of the above**
   The mean is just the total score/number of scores → 90 +… + 94)/10 → 79.9.

   The median is the score located in the middle. The middle of the set of the numbers is between 84 and 79. The average of these two scores is 81.5.

   The mode is the number that occurs the most: 78.

7. **a)**
   Multiply each t-shirt price with the number sold; add them together and divide by the total number of shirts sold.

   So Average Price = (4.50 * 8 + 13.25 * 12 + 15.50 * 4)/(8 + 12 + 4) → $10.71.

Test Your Knowledge: Exponents and Roots

1. What is $x^2y^3z^5/y^2z^{-9}$?
   a) y^5z^4.
   b) yz^4.
   c) x^2yz^{14}.
   d) $x^2y^5z^4$.
   e) xyz.

2. What is k if $(2m^3)^5 = 32m^{k+1}$?
   a) 11.
   b) 12.
   c) 13.
   d) 14.
   e) 15.

3. What is $x^5y^4z^3/x^{-3}y^2z^{-4}$?
   a) $x^6y^4z^7$.
   b) x^8yz^7.
   c) x^6yz^7.
   d) $x^8y^2z^7$.
   e) $x^6y^2z^7$.

4. Evaluate $(a^2 * a^{54} + a^{56} + (a^{58}/a^2))/a^4$.
   a) a^{56}.
   b) $3a^{56}$.
   c) $3a^{52}$.
   d) $3a^{54}$.
   e) a^{54}.

5. $9^m = 3^{-1/n}$. What is mn?
   a) .5.
   b) 2.
   c) -2.
   d) -.5.
   e) -1.

6. If $2^a*4^a = 32$, what is a?
   a) 1/3.
   b) 2/3.
   c) 1.
   d) 4/3.
   e) 5/3.

Test Your Knowledge: Exponents and Roots – Answers

1. **c)**
   $x^2y^3z^5/y^2z^{-9} = x^2y^3z^5 * y^{-2}z^9$ which gives the answer $x^2y^{(3-2)}z^{(5+9)} \rightarrow x^2yz^{14}$.

2. **d)**
   Expand $(2m^3)^5$ to give $32m^{15}$.

   So $32m^{15} = 32m^{k+1} \rightarrow k+1 = 15 \rightarrow k = 14$.

3. **d)**
   $x^5y^4z^3/x^{-3}y^2z^{-4} = x^5y^4z^3 * x^3y^{-2}z^4 = x^8y^2z^7$.

4. **c)**
   $(a^2*a^{54}+a^{56}+ (a^{58}/a^2))/a^4 = (a^{54+2}+a^{56}+a^{58-2})a^{-4} = 3a^{56}-4 = 3a^{52}$.

5. **d)**
   9^m is the same as 3^{2m}.

   So $3^{2m} = 3^{-1/n} \rightarrow 2m = -1/n \rightarrow mn = -.5$.

6. **e)**
   $2^a * 4^a$ can be re-written as $2^a * (2^2)^a$.

   $32 = 2^5$.

   Therefore, $2^{(a+2a)} = 2^5 \rightarrow 3a = 5 \rightarrow a = 5/3$.

Test Your Knowledge: Algebraic Equations

1. The number $568cd$ should be divisible by 2, 5, and 7. What are the values of the digits c and d?
   a) 56835.
   b) 56830.
   c) 56860.
   d) 56840.
   e) 56800.

2. Carla is 3 times older than her sister Megan. Eight years ago, Carla was 18 years older than her sister. What is Megan's age?
   a) 10.
   b) 8.
   c) 9.
   d) 6.
   e) 5.

3. What is the value of $f(x) = (x^2 - 25)/(x + 5)$ when $x = 0$?
   a) -1.
   b) -2.
   c) -3.
   d) -4.
   e) -5.

4. Four years from now, John will be twice as old as Sally will be. If Sally was 10 eight years ago, how old is John?
   a) 35.
   b) 40.
   c) 45.
   d) 50.
   e) 55.

5. I have some marbles. I give 25% to Vic, 20% to Robbie, 10% to Jules. I then give 6/20 of the remaining amount to my brother, and keep the rest for myself. If I end up with 315 marbles, how many did I have to begin with?
   a) 1000.
   b) 1500.
   c) 3500.
   d) 400.
   e) 500.

6. I have some marbles. I give 25% to Vic, 20% of the remainder to Robbie, 10% of that remainder to Jules and myself I then give 6/20 of the remaining amount to my brother, and keep the rest for myself. If I end up with 315 marbles, how many did I have to begin with?
   a) 800.
   b) 833.
   c) 834.
   d) 378.
   e) 500.

7. If $x = 5y + 4$, what is the value of y if $x = 29$?
    a) 33/5.
    b) 5.5.
    c) 5.
    d) 0.
    e) 29/5.

8. A bag of marbles has 8 marbles. If I buy 2 bags of marbles, how many more bags of marbles would I need to buy to have a total of at least 45 marbles?
    a) 3.
    b) 4.
    c) 5.
    d) 6.
    e) 29.

9. A factory that produces widgets wants to sell them each for \$550. It costs \$50 for the raw materials for each widget, and the startup cost for the factory was \$10000. How many widgets have to be sold so that the factory can break even?
    a) 10.
    b) 20.
    c) 30.
    d) 40.
    e) 50.

10. Expand $(3x - 4)(6 - 2x)$.
    a) $6x^2 - 6x + 8$.
    b) $-6x^2 + 26x - 24$.
    c) $6x^2 - 26x + 24$.
    d) $-6x^2 + 26x + 24$.
    e) $6x^2 + 26x - 24$.

11. If $6n + m$ is divisible by 3 and 5, which of the following numbers when added to $6n + m$ will still give a result that is divisible by 3 and 5?
    a) 4.
    b) 6.
    c) 12.
    d) 20.
    e) 60.

12. If x is negative, and $x^3/5$ and $x/5$ both give the same result, what could be the value of x?
    a) -5.
    b) -4.
    c) 3.
    d) 0.
    e) -1.

13. If $m = 3548$, and $n = 235$, then what is the value of $m * n$?
   a) 87940.
   b) 843499.
   c) 87900.
   d) 8830.
   e) 833780.

14. A ball is thrown at a speed of 30 mph. How far will it travel in 2 minutes and 35 seconds?
   a) 1.5 miles.
   b) 1.20 miles.
   c) 1.29 miles.
   d) 1.3 miles.
   e) 1.1 miles.

15. Simplify: $30(\sqrt{40} - \sqrt{60})$.
   a) $30(\sqrt{5} - \sqrt{15})$.
   b) $30(\sqrt{10} + \sqrt{15})$.
   c) $60(\sqrt{5} + \sqrt{15})$.
   d) $60(\sqrt{10} - \sqrt{15})$.
   e) 60.

16. Simplify: $30/(\sqrt{40} - \sqrt{60})$.
   a) $3(\sqrt{5} + \sqrt{15})$.
   b) $-3(\sqrt{5} - \sqrt{15})$.
   c) $-3(\sqrt{10} + \sqrt{15})$.
   d) $3(\sqrt{10} + \sqrt{15})$.
   e) $3(\sqrt{10} - \sqrt{15})$.

17. What is the least common multiple of 2, 3, 4, and 5?
   a) 30.
   b) 60.
   c) 120.
   d) 40.
   e) 50.

18. It costs \$6 to make a pen that sells for \$12. How many pens need to be sold to make a profit of \$60?
   a) 10.
   b) 6.
   c) 72.
   d) 30.
   e) 12.

Test Your Knowledge: Algebraic Equations - Answers

1. **d)**
   If the number is divisible by 2, d should be even. If the number is divisible by 5, then b has to equal 0.

   Start by making both variables 0 and dividing by the largest factor, 7.

   $56800/7 = 8114$.

   2 from 56800 is 56798, a number divisible by 2 and 7.

   Next add a multiple of 7 that turns the last number to a 0. $6 * 7 = 42$. $56798 + 42 = 56840$, which is divisible by 2, 5, and 7.

2. **c)**
   Carla's age is c; Megan's age is m. $c = 3m$; $c - 8 = m - 8 + 18$.

   Substitute $3m$ for c in equation 2 → $3m - 8 = m + 10$ → $m = 9$.

3. **e)**
   We know $(x^2 - 25) = (x + 5)(x - 5)$.

   So $(x^2 - 25)/(x + 5) = x - 5$. At $x = 0$, $f(0) = -5$.

4. **b)**
   Let j be John's age and s be Sally's age.

   $j + 4 = 2(s + 4)$.

   $s - 8 = 10$ → $s = 18$.

   So $j + 4 = 2(18 + 4)$ → $j = 40$.

5. **a)**
   If x is the number of marbles initially, then $.25x$ goes to Vic, $.2x$ goes to Robbie, and $.1x$ goes to Jules.

   The number left, x, is $(1 - .25 - .2 - .1) = .45x$.

   Of that I give 6/20 to my brother, so $6/20 * .45x$.

   I am left with $.45x(1 - (6/20)) = .315x$.

   We are also told $.315x = 315$ → $x = 1000$.

6. **c)**
Always read the question carefully! Questions 5 and 6 are similar, but they are not the same.

Let x be the original number of marbles. After Vic's share is given $.75x$ remains. After Robbie's share $.75x * .80$ remains. After Jules' share, $.75x * .8 * .9$ remains.

After I give my brother his share, $.75x * .8 * .9 * (1 - 6/20)$ remains. The remaining number = $.378x$.

We are told $.378x = 315 \rightarrow x = 833.33$. We need to increase this to the next highest number, 834, because we have part of a marble and to include it we need to have a whole marble.

7. **c)**
Replace the value of x with its value and solve the equation.

$29 = 5y + 4$.

Solving:

$29 - 4 = 5y + 4 - 4$.

$25 = 5y$ or $5y = 25$.

$\frac{5y}{5} = \frac{25}{5}$.

$y = 5$.

8. **b)**
$2(8) + x > 45$ means $x > 29$, so we need more than 29 marbles. A bag has 8 marbles, so the number of bags needed is 29/8, or 3.625. Since we need 3 bags + part of another bag, we need 4 additional bags to give at least 45 marbles.

9. **b)**
n is the number of widgets. The cost the factory incurs for making n widgets is $10000 + 50n$. The amount the factory makes by selling n widgets is $550n$.

At the break-even point, the cost incurred is equal to the amount of sales.

$10000 + 50n = 550n \rightarrow n = 20$.

10. **b)**
Use FOIL:

$(3x - 4)(6 - 2x) = 3x * 6 - 4 * 6 + 3x * (-2x) - 4 * (-2x) = 18x - 24 - 6x^2 + 8x = -6x^2 + 26x - 24$.

11. **e)**
Since $6n + m$ is divisible by 3 and 5, the new number that we get after adding a value will be divisible by 3 and 5 only if the value that we add is divisible by 3 and 5. The only number that will work from the given choices is 60.

12. e)

We are told $x^3/5 = x/5 \rightarrow x^3 = x$. The possible values are -1, 0, and 1. We are told that x is negative.

So $x = -1$.

13. e)

This problem can be done by elimination. We know that m is in the thousands, which means $x * 10^3$; and n is in the hundreds, which is $y * 10^2$. The answer will be $z * 10^5$, or 6 places in total, so we can eliminate **a)**, **c)**, and **d)**. Also we see that m ends in 8 and n ends in 5, so the answer has to end in 0 ($8 * 5 = 40$), which eliminates **b)**.

14. c)

The ball has a speed of 30 miles per hour. 30 miles per 60 minutes = .5 mile per minute; 2 minutes and 35 seconds = 2 minutes; and 35/60 minutes = 2.58 minutes.

The ball travels .5 * 2.58 = 1.29 miles.

15. d)

$$30\left(\sqrt{40} - \sqrt{60}\right) = 30\sqrt{4\,(10 - 15)} = 60\left(\sqrt{10} - \sqrt{15}\right).$$

16. c)

Multiply the numerator and the denominator by $\left(\sqrt{40} + \sqrt{60}\right)$.

So $\dfrac{30}{\left(\sqrt{40}-\sqrt{60}\right)} * \left[\dfrac{\left(\sqrt{40}+\sqrt{60}\right)}{\left(\sqrt{40}+\sqrt{60}\right)}\right] =$
$30\left(\sqrt{40} + \sqrt{60}\right)/\left(\sqrt{40} - \sqrt{60}\right)^2.$

$-3\left(\sqrt{10} + \sqrt{15}\right).$

17. b)

Find all the prime numbers that multiply to give the numbers.

For 2, prime factor is 2; for 3, prime factor is 3; for 4, prime factors are 2, 2; and for 5, prime factor is 5. Note the maximum times of occurrence of each prime and multiply these to find the least common multiple.

The LCM is 2 * 2 * 3 * 5 = 60.

18. a)

One pen sells for $12, so on the sale of a pen, the profit is 12 - 6 = 6.

In order to make $60, we need to sell 10 pens.

Test Your Knowledge: Inequalities, Literal Equations, Polynomials, and Binomials

1. If $x < 5$ and $y < 6$, then $x + y$ _?_ 11.
    a) $<$
    b) $>$
    c) $\leq$
    d) $\geq$
    e) $=$

2. Which of the following is true about the inequality $25x^2 - 40x - 32 < 22$?
    a) There are no solutions.
    b) There is a set of solutions.
    c) There is 1 solution only.
    d) There are 2 solutions.
    e) There are 3 solutions.

3. If $x - 2y > 6$, what possible values of y always have x as greater than or equal to 2?
    a) $y \geq 6$.
    b) $y \leq 0$.
    c) $y \geq -2$.
    d) $y < 2$.
    e) $y \leq 1$.

4. Find the point of intersection of the lines $x + 2y = 4$ and $3x - y = 26$.
    a) $(1, 3)$.
    b) $(8, -2)$.
    c) $(0, 2)$.
    d) $(2, -1)$.
    e) $(4, 26)$.

5. If $a + b = 2$, and $a - b = 4$, what is a?
    a) 1.
    b) 2.
    c) 3.
    d) 4.
    e) 5.

6. If $\sqrt{a} + \sqrt{b} = 2$, and $\sqrt{a} - \sqrt{b} = 3$, what is $a + b$?
    a) 4.5.
    b) 4.
    c) 5.5.
    d) 6.
    e) 6.5.

7. If $a = b + 3$, and $3b = 5a + 6$, what is $3a - 2b$?
    a) -1.5.
    b) 2.5.
    c) 3.
    d) 4.3.
    e) 5.

8. The sum of the roots of a quadratic equation is 8, and the difference is 2. What is the equation?
    a) $x^2 - 8x - 15$.
    b) $x^2 + 8x + 15$.
    c) $x^2 - 8x + 15$.
    d) $x^2 + 8x - 15$.
    e) $x^2 + 15$.

9. Solve the following system of equations: $3x + 2y = 7$ and $3x + y = 5$.
    a) $x = 2, y = 1$.
    b) $x = 2, y = 2$.
    c) $x = 1, y = 0$.
    d) $x = 1, y = 2$.
    e) $x = 1, y = 1$.

10. Nine tickets were sold for $41. If the tickets cost $4 and $5, how many $5 tickets were sold?
    a) 5.
    b) 4.
    c) 9.
    d) 6.
    e) 7.

11. Joe brought a bag of 140 M&Ms to his class of 40 students. Each boy received 2 M&Ms. Each girl received 4. How many boys were in the class?
    a) 10.
    b) 20.
    c) 30.
    d) 40.
    e) 50.

Test Your Knowledge: Inequalities, Literal Equations, Polynomials, and Binomials – Answers

1. **a)**

   Choice **a)** will always be true, while the other choices can never be true.

2. **b)**

   $25x^2 - 40x + 32 < 22 \rightarrow 25x^2 - 40x + 16 < 6 \rightarrow (5x - 4)^2 < 6 \rightarrow 5x - 4 < 6$.

   $x = 2$, so x has to be all numbers less than 2 for this inequality to work.

3. **c)**

   Rearrange equation $x > 6 + 2y$, so $2 > 6 + 2y$. Solve for y.

   $2 \geq 6 + 2y$.

   $-4 \geq 2y$, so $-2 \leq y$ or $y \geq -2$.

   (When working with inequalities, remember to reverse the sign when dividing by a negative number.)

4. **b)**

   Find the slopes first. If they are not equal, then the lines intersect. The slopes are -1/2 and 3.

   Next, solve by substitution or addition. From the first equation, $x = 4 - 2y$. Plugging this into equation 2, we get $3(4 - 2y) - y = 26 \rightarrow 7y = 12 - 26 \rightarrow y = -2$. Plug this value into either equation to find x.

   With equation 1, we get $x - 4 = 4 \rightarrow x = 8$.

5. **c)**

   Add the equations to eliminate b. $2a = 6 \rightarrow a = 3$.

6. **e)**

   Square both equations.

   Equation 1 becomes $a + 2\sqrt{ab} + b = 4$; and equation 2 becomes $a - 2\sqrt{ab} + b = 9$.

   Add the equations. $2(a + b) = 13 \rightarrow a + b = 13/2$. $13/2 = 6.5$.

7. **a)**

   Solve by substitution.

   If $a = b + 3$, and $3b = 5a + 6$, then $3b = 5(b+3) + 6$.

   If $3b - 5b - 15 = 6$, then $-2b = 21$. Therefore, $b = -10.5$.

   Now use substitution to find a. $a = b + 3$. So $a = -10.5 + 3$. Therefore, $a = -7.5$.

   Solve the equation, $3a - 2b$. $3(-7.5) - 2(-10.5) = -1.5$.

8. c)

If the roots are a and b, then $a + b = 8$ and $a - b = 2$.

Add the equations. $2a = 10$ → $a = 5$ → $b = 3$.

The factors are $(x - 5)(x - 3)$, and the equation is $x^2 - 8x + 15$.

9. d)

From the equation $3x + y = 5$, we get $y = 5 - 3x$. Substitute into the other equation. $3x + 2(5 - 3x) = 7$ → $3x + 10 - 6x = 7$ → $x = 1$. This value into either of the equations gives us $y = 2$.

10. a)

$4x + 5y = 41$, and $x + y = 9$, where x and y are the number of tickets sold.

From equation 2: $x = 9 - y$.

From equation 1: $4(9 - y) + 5y = 41$ → $36 + y = 41$ → $y = 5$.

11. a)

b is the number of boys, and g is the number of girls. So $b + g = 40$, and $2b + 4g = 140$.

To do the problem, use the substitution method. Plug $(g = 40 - b)$ into $(2b + 4g = 140)$.

$2b + 4(40 - b) = 140$ → $b = 10$.

Test Your Knowledge: Slope and Distance to Midpoint

1. If a line passes through (3, 5) and has a intercept $y = 8$, what is the equation of the line?
    a) $y = x + 8$.
    b) $y = x - 8$.
    c) $y = -x - 8$.
    d) $y = -x + 8$.
    e) $y = -x$.

2. What is the value of y in the equation $(3x - 4)^2 = 4y - 15$, if $x = 3$?
    a) 10.
    b) 2.5.
    c) -10.
    d) -2.5.
    e) 5.

3. If $y = 4x + 6y$, what is the range of y if $-10 < x \leq 5$?
    a) $-4 < y \leq 8$.
    b) $-4 < y < 8$.
    c) $8 > y > -4$.
    d) $-4 \leq y < 8$.
    e) $-4 \leq y \leq 8$.

4. If Jennifer gets three times as much allowance as Judy gets, and Judy gets $5/week, how much does Jennifer get every month?
    a) $15.
    b) $20.
    c) $30.
    d) $45.
    e) $60.

5. If $y = 8$ in the equation $5x + 9y = 3x - 6y + 5$, what is the value of x?
    a) 57.5.
    b) 60.
    c) -60.
    d) -57.5.
    e) None of the above.

6.

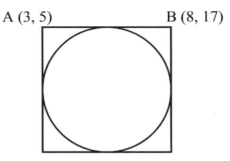

A (3, 5)   B (8, 17)

What is the area within the square whose two corners are A and B and outside the circle?
  a) 169(1-π).
  b) 169 π.
  c) 169 π /4.
  d) 169(1- π /4).
  e) 169.

7. A line with a slope of 2 passes through the point (2, 4). What is the set of coordinates where that line passes through the y intercept?
  a) (-2, 0).
  b) (0, 0).
  c) (2, 2).
  d) (4, 0).
  e) (1, 1).

8.

$$3x + 4y = 7$$
$$9x + 12y = 21$$

Determine where the above two lines intersect:
  a) $x = 4, y = 3$.
  b) $x = 12, y = 9$.
  c) $x = 1/3, y = 1/3$.
  d) Not enough information provided.
  e) There is no solution; the lines do not intersect.

9.

$$3x + 4y = 7$$
$$8x - 6y = 9$$

Are the above lines parallel or perpendicular?
  a) Perpendicular.
  b) Parallel.
  c) Neither parallel nor perpendicular.
  d) Cannot be determined.
  e) The angle at the point of intersection is 40.

10. Is the graph of the function $f(x) = -3x^2 + 4$ linear, asymptotical, symmetrical to the x axis, symmetrical to the y axis, or not symmetrical to either axis?

    a) Symmetrical to the x axis.
    b) Symmetrical to the y axis.
    c) Symmetrical to neither axis.
    d) Asymptotic.
    e) Linear.

11. Two points on a line have coordinates (3, 12) and (9, 20). What is the distance between these two points?

    a) 10.
    b) 12.
    c) 13.
    d) 8.
    e) 11.

12. In the following graph, what is the equation of line AB if line AB is perpendicular to line PQ? Point coordinates are:

$$M\ (-4, 0);\ O\ (0, 2);\ \text{and}\ N\ (0, -3).\ \text{The lines intersect at}\ (-2,1).$$

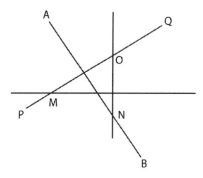

    a) $y = 2x + 3$.
    b) $y = -2x - 3$.
    c) $y = -2x - 3$.
    d) $y = x + 3$.
    e) $y = x - 4$.

13. What is the equation of a line passing through (1, 2) and (6, 12)?

    a) $y = x$.
    b) $y = 2x$.
    c) $y = x/2$.
    d) $y = 2x + 2$.
    e) $y = x - 2$.

14. What is the midpoint of the line connecting points (0, 8) and (2, 6)?

    a) (-1, 1).
    b) (2, 14).
    c) (-2, 2).
    d) (0, 1).
    e) (1, 7).

15. What is the equation of a line passing through $(1, 1)$ and $(2, 4)$?
  - a) $3y = x + 2$.
  - b) $2y = x + 3$.
  - c) $y = 3x - 2$.
  - d) $4x = y + 2$.
  - e) $y = (1/3)x + 2$.

16. Line A passes through $(0, 0)$ and $(3, 4)$. Line B passes through $(2, 6)$ and $(3, y)$. What value of y will make the lines parallel?
  - a) $20/3$.
  - b) 7.
  - c) $22/3$.
  - d) 29.
  - e) 5.

17. Line A passes through $(1, 3)$ and $(3, 4)$. Line B passes through $(3, 7)$ and $(5, y)$. What value of y will make the lines perpendicular?
  - a) 1.
  - b) 2.
  - c) 3.
  - d) 4.
  - e) 5.

18. What is the equation of line A that is perpendicular to line B, connecting $(8, 1)$ and $(10, 5)$, that intersects at $(x, 14)$?
  - a) $y = 2x - 7$.
  - b) $y = -2x + 7$.
  - c) $y = (-1/2)x + 19\frac{1}{4}$.
  - d) $y = 5x - 7$.
  - e) $y = 2x - 19\frac{1}{4}$.

Test Your Knowledge: Slope and Distance to Midpoint – Answers

1. d)

The standard form of the line equation is $y = mx + b$. We need to find slope m.

$m = (y_2 - y_1)/(x_2 - x_1)$ → $m = (5 - 8)/(3 - 0)$ → $m = -1$.

Therefore the equation is $y = -x + 8$.

2. a)

At $x = 3$, $((3 * 3) - 4)^2 = 4y - 15$.

$(9 - 4)^2 = 4y - 15$.

$25 = 4y - 15$.

$40 = 4y$.

$y = 10$.

3. d)

Rearrange the equation and combine like terms. $-5y = 4x$.

At $x = -10$, $y = 8$. At $x = 5$, $y = -4$. The range of y is therefore $-4 \leq y < 8$.

4. e)

If Judy gets x dollars, then Jennifer gets $3x$ in a week. In a month, Jennifer will then get $4 * 3x$.

If Judy gets $5 per week, then Jennifer gets $60 in a month.

5. d)

Combine like terms.

$5x + 9y = 3x - 6y + 5$ → $2x = -15y + 5$ → $x = -57.5$ when $y = 8$.

6. d)

First we need to find the length of side AB.

$AB = \sqrt{(17 - 5)^2 + (8 - 3)^2} = 13$.

If $AB = 13$, then $A_{square} = 13^2 = 169$.

AB is also the diameter of the circle. $A_{circle} \, \pi \, (d^2/4) = 169 \, \pi /4$.

The area outside the circle and within the square is: $A_{square} - A_{circle} = 169(1 - \pi /4)$.

7. **b)**

The slope of the line is given as $m = (y_2 - y_1)/(x_2 - x_1)$, where (x_1, y_1) and (x_2, y_2) are two points which the line passes through.

The y intercept is the point where the graph intersects the y axis, so $x = 0$ at this point.

Plug in the values of m, etc.; we get $2 = (4 - y)/(2 - 0) \rightarrow y = 0$.

8. **e)**

While it is tempting to solve this system of simultaneous equations to find the values of x and y, the first thing to do is to see whether the lines intersect. To do this, compare the slopes of the two lines by putting the lines into the standard form, $y = mx + b$, where m is the slope.

By rearranging, equation 1 becomes $y = 7/4 - 3x/4$; and equation 2 becomes $y = 21/12 - 9x/12$.

The slope of line 1 is -3/4, and the slope of line 2 is -9/12, which reduces to -3/4. Since the slopes are equal, the lines are parallel and do not intersect.

9. **a)**

Find the slopes by rearranging the two equations into the form $y = mx + b$.

Equation 1 becomes $y = -3x/4 + 7/4$ and equation 2 becomes $y = 8x/6 - 9/6$.

So $m_1 = -3/4$ and $m_2 = 8/6 = 4/3$. We see that m_1 is the negative inverse of m_2, so line 1 is perpendicular to line 2.

10. **b)**

Find the values of the y coordinate for different values of the x coordinate (example, [-3, +3]). We get the following chart:

x	y
-3	-23
-2	-8
-1	1
0	4
1	1
2	-8
3	-23

From these values, we see the graph is symmetrical to the y axis.

11. **a)**

Distance $s = \sqrt{(x_2 - x_1)^2 + (y_2 - y_1)^2} \rightarrow s = \sqrt{(9 - 3)^2 + (20 - 12)^2} = \sqrt{36 + 64} = 10$.

12. **b)**

$y = mx + b$; m is the slope and b is the y intercept.

Calculate m for line AB using the given points (0, -3) and (-2, 1). $m = (-3 - 1)/(0 - (-2)) = -2$. The y intercept is -3 (from point set given), so $y = -2x - 3$.

110

13. b)

First, find the slope, $(y_2 \text{-} y_1)/(x_2 \text{-} x_1)$ ➜ slope $= (12 - 2)/(6 - 1) = 2$.

Next, use the slope and a point to find the value of b.

In the standard line equation, $y = mx + b$, use the point $(6, 12)$ to get $12 = (2 * 6) + b$ ➜ $b = 0$.

The equation of the line is $y = 2x$.

14. e)

The midpoint is at $(x_1 + x_2)/2, (y_1 + y_2)/2 = (1,7)$.

15. c)

Slope $= (y_2 - y_1)/(x_2 - x_1) = 3$. Plug one of the coordinates into $y = mx + b$ to find the value of b.

$1 = 3(1) + b$ ➜ $b = - 2$.

The equation of the line is $y = 3x - 2$.

16. c)

Calculate the slope of each line. Slope of line A $= 4/3$; and slope of line B $= y - 6$.

The slopes of the line have to be the same for the lines to be parallel.

$4/3 = y - 6$ ➜ $4 = 3y - 18$ ➜ $y = 22/3$.

17. c)

The slope of line A $= \frac{1}{2}$; and the slope of line B $= (y - 7)/2$.

The product of the slopes has to equal -1.

$(1/2)[(y - 7)/2] = -1$ ➜ $(y - 7)/4 = -1$ ➜ $y = 3$.

18. c)

Slope$_b = (5 - 1)/(10 - 8) = 2$. The slope of line A is -1/2.

To find the intercept of line B, use $y = mx + b$.

$5 = (2)(10) + b$, so $b = -7$. Equation of line B is $y = 2x - 7$.

Find intersect x, using the given y coordinate. $14 = 2x - 7$; $x = 10.5$.

Find the intercept of line A using the coordinates of intersection.

$14 = (-1/2)(10.5) + b$. $b = 19\frac{1}{4}$.

The equation of line A is $y = - (1/2)x + 19\frac{1}{4}$.

Test Your Knowledge: Absolute Value Equations

1. Factor $x^2 + 2x - 15$.
    a) $(x - 1)(x + 15)$.
    b) $(x - 3)(x - 5)$.
    c) $(x + 3)(x + 5)$.
    d) $(x + 3)(x - 5)$.
    e) $(x - 3)(x + 5)$.

2. Car A starts at 3:15 PM and travels straight to its destination at a constant speed of 50 mph. If it arrives at 4:45 PM, how far did it travel?
    a) 70 miles.
    b) 75 miles.
    c) 65 miles.
    d) 40 miles.
    e) 105 miles.

3. What are the roots of the equation $2x^2 + 14x = 0$?
    a) 0 and 7.
    b) 0 and -7.
    c) 14 and 0.
    d) 2 and 14.
    e) Cannot be determined.

4. If $f(x) = 2x^2 + 3x$, and $g(x) = x + 4$, what is $f[g(x)]$?
    a) $x^2 + 19x + 44$.
    b) $2x^2 + 19x + 44$.
    c) $4x^2 + 35x + 76$.
    d) $x^2 + 8x + 16$.
    e) None of the above.

5. If $|x + 4| = 2$, what are the values of x?
    a) 2 and 6.
    b) -2 and -6.
    c) -2.
    d) -6.
    e) 0.

6. The sale of an item can be written as a function of price: $s = 3p + c$, where s is the amount in sales, p is the price per item, and c is a constant value. If the sales generated are $20 at a price of $5 for the item, then what should the price be to generate $50 in sales?
    a) $10.
    b) $15.
    c) $20.
    d) $16.
    e) $14.

7. If $f(n) = 2n + 3\sqrt{n}$, where n is a positive integer, what is $f[g(5)]$ if $g(m) = m - 4$?
   a) 1.
   b) 2.
   c) 3.
   d) 4.
   e) 5.

8. If $f(x) = (x + 2)^2$, and $-4 \leq x \leq 4$, what is the minimum value of $f(x)$?
   a) 0.
   b) 1.
   c) 2.
   d) 3.
   e) 4.

9. If $f(x) = (x + 2)^2$, and $0 \leq x \leq 4$, what is the minimum value of $f(x)$?
   a) 1.
   b) 2.
   c) 3.
   d) 4.
   e) 5.

10. What is $x^2 - 9$ divided by $x - 3$?
   a) $x - 3$.
   b) $x + 3$.
   c) x.
   d) $x - 1$.
   e) 6.

11. An equation has two roots: 5 and -8. What is a possible equation?
   a) $x^2 - 3x + 40$.
   b) $x^2 - 3x - 40$.
   c) $x^2 + x + 40$.
   d) $x^2 + 3x - 40$.
   e) $2x^2 - 3x + 40$.

12. In an ant farm, the number of ants grows every week according to the formula
   $N = 100 + 2^w$, where w is the number of weeks elapsed. How many ants will the colony have after 5 weeks?
   a) 115.
   b) 125.
   c) 135.
   d) 132.
   e) 233.

13. Find the values of x that validate the following equation: $[(4x+5)^2 - (40x+25)]^{1/2} + 3|x| - 14 = 0.$
   a) 2, 14.
   b) -2, 14.
   c) 2, -14.
   d) -2, -14.
   e) No solution.

14. If $|x| = 4$ and $|y| = 5$, what are the values of $|x+y|$?
   a) -1, -9.
   b) -1, -9.
   c) -1, 9.
   d) 1, 9.
   e) $1 < |x+y| < 9$.

15. If $y = |x|$, what is the range of y?
   a) $y < 0$.
   b) $0 < y < x$.
   c) $y > 0$.
   d) $y \geq 0$.
   e) $y > x$.

Test Your Knowledge: Absolute Value Equations – Answers

1. **a)**
   The constant term is -15. The factors should multiply to give -15 and add to give 2.
   The numbers -3 and 5 satisfy both, $(x - 3)(x + 5)$.

2. **b)**
   The time between 3:15 PM and 4:45 PM = 1.5 hours. $1.5 * 50 = 75$.

   Reminder: half an hour is written as .5 of an hour, not .3 of an hour, even though on a clock a half hour is 30 minutes.

3. **b)**
   Rearrange, reduce, and factor.

   $2x^2 + 14x + 0 = 0$.

   $2(x^2 + 7x + 0) = 0$.

   $(x + 7)(x + 0)$.

   $x = 0$, or -7.

4. **b)**
   Substitute g(x) for every x in $f(x)$.

   $f[g((x + 4))] = 2(x + 4)^2 + 3(x + 4) = 2x^2 + 16x + 32 + 3x + 12 = 2x^2 + 19x + 44$.

5. **b)**
   Two solutions: $(x + 4) = 2$ and $-(x + 4) = 2$.

   Or $x + 4 = 2$, $x = -2$.

   And $x + 4 = -2$, $x = -6$.

6. **b)**
   Find the value of the constant by plugging in the given information.

   $20 = 3 * 5 + c \rightarrow c = 5$.

   Now use the value of c and the new value of s to find p. $50 = 3p + 5 \rightarrow p = 15$.

7. **e)**
   g(5) = 5 - 4 = 1. $f[g(5)] = 2 * 1 + 3\sqrt{1} = 5$.

8. **a)**
   From the domain of x, the lowest value of x is -4, and the highest value is 4. We are tempted to think that $f(x)$ will have the least value at $x = -4$: $f(-4) = 4$. However, $f(x)$ is equal to a squared value, so the lowest value of $f(x)$ is 0. This happens at $x = -2$.

9. d)

The lowest value of $f(x)$ can be 0, since $f(x)$ is equal to a squared value, but, for $f(x) = 0$, x must equal -2. That is outside the domain of x. The least value of $f(x) = 4$.

10. b)

$x^2 - 9$ can be factored into $(x + 3)$ and $(x - 3)$.

$[(x + 3)(x - 3)]/(x - 3) = x + 3$.

11. d)

If the roots are 5 and -8, then the factors are $(x - 5)(x + 8)$. Multiply the factors to get the equation.

$x^2 + 3x - 40$.

12. d)

After 5 weeks, the number of ants $= 100 + 32$, or 132.

13. a)

Expand the equation:

$[16x^2 + 40x + 25 - 40x - 25]^{1/2} + 3|x| - 14 = 0$.

$(16x^2)^{1/2} + 3|x| - 14 = 0$.

$4x + 3|x| - 14 = 0$.

$3|x| = 14 - 4x$.

$|x| = \dfrac{14}{3} - \dfrac{4x}{3}$ $x = \dfrac{14}{3} - \dfrac{4x}{3} = 2$ $x = -\dfrac{14}{3} - \dfrac{4x}{3} = 14$.

14. d)

$x = 4$ and $y = 5$, $|x + y| = 9$.

$x = -4$ and $y = 5$, $|x + y| = 1$.

$x = 4$ and $y = -5$, $|x + y| = 1$.

$x = -4$ and $y = -5$, $|x + y| = 9$.

15. d)

The absolute value of x can be at least a 0, and is otherwise positive regardless of the value of x.

$y \geq 0$.

Test Your Knowledge: Geometry

1. If the sides of a triangle have lengths of 3, 4, and 5 feet, what is its area in square feet?
   a) 6 square feet.
   b) 7 square feet.
   c) 4 square feet.
   d) 5 square feet.
   e) 8 square feet.

2. In the following figure, where AE bisects line BC, and angles AEC and AEB are both right angles, what is the length of AB?
   a) 1 cm.
   b) 2 cm.
   c) 3 cm.
   d) 4 cm.
   e) 5 cm.

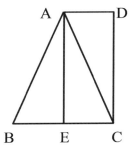

BC = 6 cm
AD = 3 cm
CD = 4 cm

3. In the following triangle, if AB = 6 and BC = 8, what should the length of CA be to make triangle ABC a right triangle?
   a) 4.
   b) 7.
   c) 8.
   d) 9.
   e) 10.

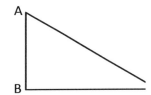

4. In the following circle there is a square with an area of 36 cm². What is the area outside the square, but within the circle?
   a) 18π cm².
   b) 18π - 30 cm².
   c) 18π - 36 cm².
   d) 18 cm².
   e) -18 cm².

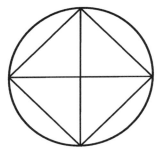

5. The length of a rectangle is 4 times its width. If the width of the rectangle is $5 - x$ inches, and the perimeter of the rectangle is 30 inches, what is x?
   a) 1.
   b) 2.
   c) 3.
   d) 4.
   e) 5.

6. Two sides of a triangle have a ratio AC:BC = 5:4. The length of AB on a similar triangle = 24. What is the actual value of AC for the larger triangle?
   a) 10.
   b) 14.4.
   c) 35.
   d) 40.
   e) 50.

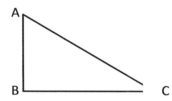

7. If a circle's diameter is doubled, the area increases by what factor?
   a) 1 time.
   b) 2 times.
   c) 3 times.
   d) 4 times.
   e) 5 times.

8. In the following triangle PQR, what is the measure of angle A?
   a) 145^0.
   b) 140^0.
   c) 70^0.
   d) 50^0.
   e) 40^0.

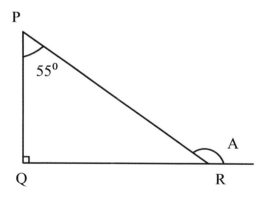

Test Your Knowledge: Geometry – Answers

1. **a)**
   The Pythagorean triple (special right triangle property) means the two shorter sides form a right triangle.

   $1/2bh$ = A. So, $(1/2)(3)(4) = 6$.

2. **e)**
   $AB^2 = AC^2 = AD2 + CD^2 \rightarrow AB^2 = 3^2 + 4^2 \rightarrow AB = 5$.

3. **e)**
   As per the Pythagorean Theorem, a hypotenuse's square is equivalent to the sum of the leg's two sides.

   $AB^2 + BC^2 = AC^2 \rightarrow AC^2 = 36 + 64 \rightarrow AC = 10$.

4. **c)**
   If the area of the square is 36 cm^2, then each side is 6 cm. If we look at the triangle made by half the square, that diagonal would be the hypotenuse of the triangle, and its length = $\sqrt{6^2 + 6^2} = 6\sqrt{2}$.

   This hypotenuse is also the diameter of the circle, so the radius of the circle is $3\sqrt{2}$.

   The area of the circle = $A = \pi r^2 = 18\pi$.

   The area outside the square, but within the circle is 18π -36.

5. **b)**
   Perimeter of a rectangle = $2(l + w)$. Width = $5 - x$; and length = $4(5 - x)$.

   Perimeter = $2(l * w) = 30 \rightarrow 2(20 - 4x + 5 - x) = 30 \rightarrow -10x = -20 \rightarrow x = 2$.

6. **d)**
   Side AC = 5, and side BC = 4. The Pythagorean triple is 3:4:5, so side AB = 3.

   Because the other triangle is similar, the ratio of all sides is constant. AB:AB = 3:24. The ratio factor is 8.

   AC of the larger triangle = 5 * 8 = 40.

7. **d)**
   The area of a circle = πr^2.

   If the diameter is doubled, then the radius is also doubled.

   The new area = $\pi * (2r)^2 = 4 * \pi * r^2$. The area increases four times.

8. **a)**
   $\angle P = 55^0$. $\angle Q = 90^0$. $\angle R = 180 - (55 + 90) = 35^0$, and $\angle A = 180 - 35 = 145^0$.

Test Your Knowledge: Fundamental Counting Principle, Permutations, Combinations

1. The wardrobe of a studio contains 4 hats, 3 suits, 5 shirts, 2 pants, and 3 pairs of shoes. How many different ways can these items be put together?
    a) 60.
    b) 300.
    c) 360.
    d) 420.
    e) 500.

2. For lunch, you have a choice between chicken fingers or cheese sticks for an appetizer; turkey, chicken, or veal for the main course; cake or pudding for dessert; and either Coke or Pepsi for a beverage. How many choices of possible meals do you have?
    a) 16.
    b) 24.
    c) 34.
    d) 36.
    e) 8.

3. For an office job, I need to pick 3 candidates out of a pool of 5. How many choices do I have?
    a) 60.
    b) 20.
    c) 10.
    d) 30.
    e) 50.

4. A contractor is supposed to choose 3 tiles out of a stack of 5 tiles to make as many patterns as possible. How many different patterns can he make?
    a) 10.
    b) 20.
    c) 30.
    d) 40.
    e) 60.

5. I have chores to do around the house on a weekend. There are 5 chores I must complete by the end of the day. I can choose to do them in any order, so long as they are all completed. How many choices do I have?
    a) 5.
    b) 25.
    c) 32.
    d) 3125.
    e) 120.

6. Next weekend, I have more chores to do around the house. There are 5 chores I must complete by the end of the day. I can choose to do any 2 of them in any order, and then do any 2 the next day again in any order, and then do the remaining 1 the following day. How many choices do I have?
    a) 20.
    b) 6.
    c) 120.
    d) 130.
    e) 25.

7. A certain lottery play sheet has 10 numbers from which 5 have to be chosen. How many different ways can I pick the numbers?
    a) 150.
    b) 250.
    c) 252.
    d) 143.
    e) 278.

8. At a buffet, there are 3 choices for an appetizer, 6 choices for a beverage, and 3 choices for an entrée. How many different ways can I select food from all the food choices?
    a) 12.
    b) 27.
    c) 36.
    d) 42.
    e) 54.

9. If there is a basket of 10 assorted fruits, and I want to pick out 3 fruits, how many combinations of fruits do I have to choose from?
    a) 130.
    b) 210.
    c) 310.
    d) 120.
    e) 100.

10. How many ways can I pick 3 numbers from a set of 10 numbers?
    a) 720.
    b) 120.
    c) 180.
    d) 150.
    e) 880.

Test Your Knowledge: Fundamental Counting Principle, Permutations, Combinations

1. c)

The number of ways = 4 * 3 * 5 * 2 * 3 = 360.

2. b)

Multiply the possible number of choices for each item from which you can choose.

2 * 3 * 2 * 2 = 24.

3. c)

This is a combination problem. The order of the candidates does not matter.

The number of combinations = 5!/3!(5 - 3)! = 5 * 4/2 * 1 = 10.

4. e)

This is a permutation problem. The order in which the tiles are arranged is counted.

The number of patterns = 5!/(5 - 3)! = 5 * 4 * 3 = 60.

5. e)

This is a permutation problem. The order in which the chores are completed matters.

$^5P_5$ = 5!/(5 - 5)! = 5! = 5 * 4 * 3 * 2 * 1 = 120.

6. c)

#Choices$_{today}$ = $^5P_2$ = 5!/(5 - 2)! = 5 * 4 = 20.

#Choices$_{tomorrow}$ = $^3P_2$ = 3!/1! = 6.

#Choices$_{day3}$ = 1.

The total number of permutations = 20 * 6 * 1 = 120.

7. c)

This is a combinations problem. The order of the numbers is not relevant.

$^{10}n_5$ = 10!/5!(10 - 5)! = 10 * 9 * 8 * 7 * 6/5 * 4 * 3 * 2 * 1 = 252.

8. e)

There are 3 ways to choose an appetizer, 6 ways to choose a beverage, and 3 ways to choose an entrée. The total number of choices = 3 * 6 * 3 = 54.

9. d)

$^{10}C_3$ = 10!/(3!(10 - 3)!) = 10!/(3! * 7!) = 10 * 9 * 8/3 * 2 * 1 = 120.

10. b)

$^{10}P_4$ = 10!/3!(10 - 3)! = 10 * 9 * 8/3 * 2 * 1 = 120.

Test Your Knowledge: Ratios, Proportions, Rate of Change

1. A class has 50% more boys than girls. What is the ratio of boys to girls?
    a) 4:3.
    b) 3:2.
    c) 5:4.
    d) 10:7.
    e) 7:5.

2. A car can travel 30 miles on 4 gallons of gas. If the gas tank has a capacity of 16 gallons, how far can it travel if the tank is ¾ full?
    a) 120 miles.
    b) 90 miles.
    c) 60 miles.
    d) 55 miles.
    e) 65 miles.

3. The profits of a company increase by $5000 every year for five years and then decrease by $2000 for the next two years. What is the average rate of change in the company profit for that seven-year period?
    a) $1000/year.
    b) $2000/year.
    c) $3000/year.
    d) $4000/year.
    e) $5000/year.

4. A bag holds 250 marbles. Of those marbles, 40% are red, 30% are blue, 10% are green, and 20% are black. How many marbles of each color are present in the bag?
    a) Red = 90; Blue = 80; Green = 30; Black = 40.
    b) Red = 80; Blue = 60; Green = 30; Black = 80.
    c) Red = 100; Blue = 75; Green = 25; Black = 50.
    d) Red = 100; Blue = 70; Green = 30; Black = 50.
    e) Red = 120; Blue = 100; Green = 10; Black = 20.

5. Two students from a student body of 30 boys and 50 girls will be selected to serve on the school disciplinary committee. What is the probability that first a boy will be chosen, and then a girl?
    a) 1/1500.
    b) 1500/6400.
    c) 1500/6320.
    d) 1.
    e) 30/50.

6. If number n, divided by number m, gives a result of .5, what is the relationship between n and m?
    a) n is twice as big as m.
    b) m is three times as big as n.
    c) n is a negative number.
    d) m is a negative number.
    e) n is ½ of m.

7. In a fruit basket, there are 10 apples, 5 oranges, 5 pears, and 6 figs. If I select two fruits, what is the probability that I will first pick a pear and then an apple?
    a) .07.
    b) .08.
    c) 1/13.
    d) 13.
    e) 5.

8. In a fruit basket, there are 3 apples, 5 oranges, 2 pears, and 2 figs. If I pick out two fruits, what is the probability that I will pick a fig first and then an apple?
    Round to the nearest 100th.
    a) .04.
    b) .05.
    c) .06.
    d) .03.
    e) .02.

9. If x workers can make p toys in c days, how many toys can y workers make in d days if they work at the same rate?
    a) cp/qx.
    b) cq/px.
    c) cqy/px.
    d) pdy/cx.
    e) qy/px.

10. If a car travels 35 miles on a gallon of gas, how far will it travel on 13 gallons of gas?
    a) 189 miles.
    b) 255 miles.
    c) 335 miles.
    d) 455 miles.
    e) 500 miles.

Test Your Knowledge: Ratios, Proportions, Rate of Change

1. **b)**
    The ratio of boys to girls is 150:100, or 3:2.

2. **b)**
    A full tank has 16 gallons → 3/4 of the tank = 12 gallons. The car can travel 30 miles on 4 gallons, so 12 gallons would take the car 12 * 30/4 = 90 miles.

3. **c)**
    Average Rate of Change = the change in value/change in time = (total profit – initial profit)/change in time. Initial profit = 0; change in time = 7 years.

    Increase = 5000 * 5 = 25000; decrease = 2000 * 2 = 4000; total profit = 25000 - 4000 = 21000.

    (21000 - 0)/7 years = $3000/year.

4. **c)**
    Total number of marbles = 250.

    #red marbles = 250 * 40/100 = 250 * .4 = 100.

    #blue marbles = 250 * .3 = 75.

    #green marbles = 250 * .1 = 25.

    #black marbles = 250 * .2 = 50.

5. **c)**
    The probability of selecting a boy from the entire group = 30:80.

    The probability of selecting a girl from the remaining group = 50:79.

    The probability of selecting a boy and a girl is (30:80) * (50:79) = 1500:6320.

6. **e)**
    If n/m = .5, then n = .5m, or n = ½ of m.

7. **c)**
    The total number of fruit = 26.

    The probability of picking a pear = 5:26.

    The probability of picking an apple = 10:25.

    The probability of picking a pear and an apple = 5:26 * 10:25 = 50:650 = 1:13.

8. **b)**

The total number of fruit = 12.

The probability of picking a fig = 2;12.

The probability of picking an apple = 3;11.

The probability of picking a fig and an apple = 2;12 * 3;11 = 6;132 = .045.

Round up to .05.

9. **d)**

The overall rate for x workers = the number of toys/ the number of days, p/c. The number of toys one worker makes per day (rate) = p/cx. If q is the number of toys y workers make, and the rates are equal, then the number of toys made = the rate x.

The number of days * the number of workers gives us $q = p/cx$ (dy), so:

$q = pdy/cx$.

10. **d)**

The distance travelled = $(35/1)(13) = 455$ miles.

Resources and Help

You may have read through some of this book and thought, "Uh oh...I don't really remember learning that." That's okay! You are not alone. (It was the Math section, wasn't it? That's where most people forget material.) Not to worry, try these resources for additional help.

- **Purple Math** @ www.purplemath.com
  Purple math is a fantastic resource for intensive help on individual mathematic concepts. The website offers many extended tutorials in each of the subjects listed in the math section of this book. Practice questions are available here, so use them if you need more opportunities to improve.

- **Khan Academy** @ www.khanacademy.org
  Khan Academy is a great resource for math questions, as well as for tutorials related to individual concepts listed in this book. Simply visit the website and scroll down to the concepts you want to learn about.

- **Flash Cards**
  While flash cards don't work for most word problems, they can be valuable for improving your mental math abilities. Trivium Test Prep offers "brain trainer" math flash-cards to work on speed and accuracy in answering basic math questions. Flash cards help improve your mental math ability, as well as review concepts you must be familiar with for success on the exam. Visit our website under the "Product" menu to find the cards.

Final Thoughts

In the end, we know that you will be successful in taking the CHSPE. Although the road ahead may at times be challenging, if you continue your hard work and dedication (just like you are doing to prepare right now!), you will find that your efforts will pay off.

If you are struggling after reading this book and following our guidelines, we sincerely hope that you will take note of our advice and seek additional help. Start by asking friends about the resources that they are using. If you are still not reaching the score you want, consider getting the help of a tutor.

If you are on a budget and cannot afford a private tutoring service, there are plenty of independent tutors, including college students who are proficient in CHSPE subjects. You don't have to spend thousands of dollars to afford a good tutor or review course.

We wish you the best of luck and happy studying. Most importantly, we hope you enjoy your coming years – after all, you put a lot of work into getting there in the first place.

Sincerely,
The Trivium Team

Made in the USA
San Bernardino, CA
18 January 2016